MW00855841

Descent Into Chaos

The Doomed Expedition to Low's Gully

Also from Brassey's:

MAKEPEACE-WARNE
Brassey's Companion to the British Army

LAFFIN
The World in Conflict: War Annual 7

MCINNES
Hot War, Cold War
The British Army's Way in Warfare 1945–95

CENTRE FOR DEFENCE STUDIES
Brassey's Defence Yearbook 1996

Descent Into Chaos

The Doomed Expedition to Low's Gully

RICHARD CONNAUGHTON

Brassey's
London • Washington

First English Edition 1996

UK editorial offices: Brassey's, 33 John Street, London WC1N 2AT
UK orders: Marston Book Services, PO Box 269, Oxford OX14 4SD

North American orders: Brassey's Inc., PO Box 960, Herndon, VA 22070, USA

Library of Congress Cataloging in Publication Data
available

British Library Cataloguing in Publication Data
A catalogue record for this book is available from the British Library

ISBN 1 85753 147 7 Hardcover

Typeset by Solidus (Bristol) Ltd
Printed in Great Britain by Bookcraft (Bath) Ltd.

Contents

List of Plates

List of Maps

Acknowledgements

When I first became acquainted with the Low's Gully saga and heard the accounts which emerged, I thought 'this seems odd'. Curiosity took me off in search of the truth of the matter. I am most grateful to all those people who allowed me to interview or quote them, to the Rt Hon the Lord Hunt, Major General Keith Spacie and Hugh McManners for their expert opinion, to Steven Johnson for his illustrations, and to the Editors of the following newspapers from which I have either quoted or received material assistance: *Borneo Mail, Daily Mail, Hong Kong Eastern Express, Gloucestershire Echo, Sabah Daily Express, Sunday Times* and the *Western Morning News.*

Preface

When the news of the *débâcle* of Low's Gully first hit the headlines, I remember thinking how funny it was – funny odd, that is, not funny amusing. Here we had half the members of a ten-man expedition – mostly fit and able young British non-commissioned officers – emerging from a five-mile-long hellhole which falls precipitously away from Borneo's haunted mountain, Mount Kinabalu. Yet the substance of the news related neither to their emergence, barely alive, nor to their substantial achievement in being the first to conquer Low's Gully. The emphasis of the news during March 1994 rested upon the remainder of the team who, at the time, were supposedly lost in the same gully. It was the media's description of those lost which struck home as the principal oddity in what transpired to be an attempt to be the first to achieve something described as seriously difficult. The lost included two relatively senior British army officers with an average age of 50 and three novice Hong Kong Chinese storemen and guards, average age 27, from the British Army's stores depot in Hong Kong. The other oddity to ponder was, why had they broken the golden rule for such expeditions – never split up?

The details of the subsequent rescue attempt by Malaysian and British servicemen as well as local people, became a daily feature in the newspapers and on television. Then, seemingly against all odds, the five were found alive and reasonably well. Shortly afterwards, one of the officers sold the details contained in his diary to the London *Daily Mail* for what was understood to have been £25,000 (US$37,500) plus his solicitor's fees. Some of the contents of that diary proved to be savage, vitriolic, unprecedented and in part untrue. The officer publicly blamed the members of the group of non-commissioned officers who were the first to emerge, as well as the unsuspecting Chinese soldiers, who had asked to be excused from the exercise as soon as its degree of difficulty dawned upon them. The attack on the locally-enlisted Chinese soldiers gave rise to protestations and an outburst of public indignation in Hong Kong.

The same officer who sold his diary also sold his video film for a sum believed to be in excess of £25,000 (US$37,500). Then, at a news conference in York, at what should have been a harmonizing public relations exercise, the other officer strayed from what was believed to have been a pre-rehearsed script by blaming the non-commissioned officers for his group's predicament. One of the non-commissioned officers present wisely counselled the awaiting of the findings of a Board of Inquiry due to convene on 24 April 1994 before making hasty judgements. That observation proved to be sound for, after the outline of the Board's deliberations had been released, three non-commissioned officers received the General Officer Commanding's commendation for their conduct during the exercise. The Board's verdict went against the officers. The view was taken that during part of the expedition, the leader's judgement and leadership was flawed.

The irony of this state of affairs was that significant financial rewards were bestowed certainly upon one of the officers who had failed, rather than upon those who had completed a mission which for a number of the team members proved to be over-ambitious. What left a clinging odour about this exchange of rewards was the cost of the rescue to both the Malaysian and British governments and the risks taken by the rescuers. The cashing in on what had been a foolhardy and, for those involved, failed expedition, was never the major issue. The issue revolved around a betrayal of subordinates associated with that financial gain.

The Army's announcement that they were not going to make the detailed findings of the Board of Inquiry available to the public meant that the only possible descriptions of the turn of events were likely to come from the pens of those involved. The two officers were in by far the strongest position to tell their half of the story as they would wish to see it presented. For example, at the subsequent Board of Inquiry, individual accounts of what had happened, taken from the debriefing sessions, were distributed among the team. When one member noted that the accounts of the two officers were not among the testimonies, he asked for them. 'But I was told that, since they were not debriefed, there was no record to hand over.' The fact that they were there, albeit as architects and participants in this ignoble and failed venture, meant that any book arising would yet again set the cash registers ringing. To my mind, theirs would not necessarily be a comprehensive illumination of events, nor would it necessarily represent natural justice. Their book *SOS* did emerge and gave rise to great anxiety and dismay among the officers' juniors. 'I expected them to put the truth in the book: they didn't lie but they were economical and selective with the truth that they used', said Sergeant Mann. Major Foster, the deputy team leader who left the Army on 1 April 1995, was in the best position to promote the book. It was in May 1995, at a book-signing session in Waterstone's Bookshop, New George Street, Plymouth, that a confrontation occurred between Richard Mayfield, the expedition's climbing expert and Major Foster. Mayfield's principal objection was that the team leader, Lieutenant Colonel Robert Neill, and Foster, both in the book and in a BBC emergency-oriented programme, suggested that Mayfield and his fellow junior NCOs in the advance party had left Neill's and Foster's group to die. 'If we hadn't got out,' insisted Mayfield, 'no one would have survived. According to the book and TV programme we left them to die, which is a complete fallacy.'

I read *SOS* and certainly, the first page painted Major Foster as an heroic, latter-day Captain Oates going off alone into the jungle to bring help for the other four emaciated members of his team. His team leader did not think he would make it. So, immediately, from page one, the contradictions had begun. Foster insisted *he* wrote the book, 'to set the record straight'. Moreover, he defended his position by saying that the Ministry of Defence was quite happy with the book. The persistent protest of the junior NCOs had fallen on stony ground but, nevertheless, their objections deserved investigation. Was Foster a hero or a charlatan? Certainly, in his diary, Neill wrote that Foster was 'a bloody good man'. The team leader's apparent passivity after the rescue is due to his being a still serving regular officer. Foster was a territorial army officer who was a financial adviser by profession. He was not bound by the restraints affecting Lieutenant Colonel Neill. I therefore decided to study the whole Kinabalu venture with an open mind, from its origins to its course and then to its aftermath. My search for the truth took me around the United Kingdom, to Hong Kong and to Sabah, Eastern Malaysia. What I ended up producing is a story in which the facts are allowed to speak for themselves. I believe that which follows is as close as it is possible to get to a truly balanced account of what became the notorious *Descent Into Chaos.*

1
Origins

Sabah, Eastern Malaysia, Thursday, 24 March 1994

Two European men in their mid-forties to mid-fifties sat out in tattered clothes and trainers in front of a cave among a clump of large, rounded boulders. Deep in concentration, their attention focused upon something small that lay between them. Their slow, almost mechanical movements and their run-down, dishevelled appearance – the darker man with the beard appeared to be in the worst state, with pronounced hollow cheeks and sunken eyes – underlined a shared weariness born of despair. The grey-haired, bearded elder of the two seemed to be in a marginally better condition. On occasion, he took his eyes from the ground, searching for the sky through a rolling mist squeezed between a formidable terrain and low clouds. He tilted his head to the left, then to the right, apparently in anticipation of hearing something. Then, with a sigh of resignation, he returned his attention to the pocket chess set on the ground. With a hint of deference he said to his colleague, 'your move Robert'.

Close by, but distinctly separate, a group of three men were sitting on sodden ground, looking frozen, disconsolate and utterly dejected. The three were showing signs of advanced malnutrition. A closer examination would reveal them to be Chinese men in their mid-twenties. All five men had become trapped in a ravine with unscalable walls. Above the river running close by, there thundered a 400ft waterfall while another of similar proportions fell away from where they were sitting, effectively ensnaring them within a circle of unnegotiable obstacles. Their cry for help lay spelt out in a large SOS constructed of rocks lying atop a flat boulder. All five were members of the British army, the two Europeans a Lieutenant Colonel and

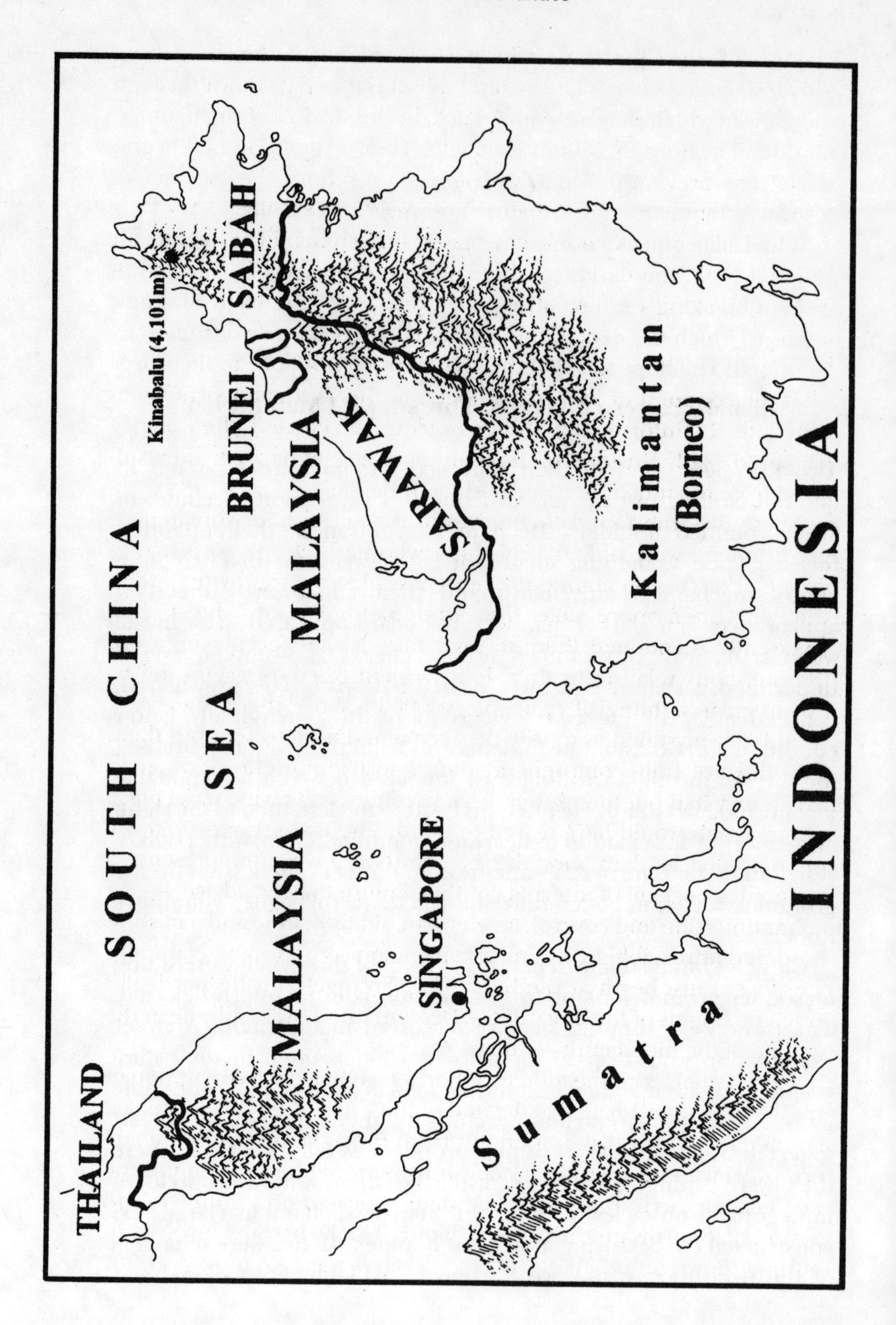
THAILAND
SOUTH CHINA
SEA
MALAYSIA
SINGAPORE
Sumatra
INDONESIA
Kalimantan
(Borneo)
SARAWAK
MALAYSIA
BRUNEI
SABAH
Kinabalu (4,101m)

Major, while the Chinese were locally-enlisted men in the Hong Kong Military Service Corps. The group had set out to pass down through the gully in which they were now stuck, in the shadow of the haunted mountain of Borneo, Mount Kinabalu. Their expedition had begun thirty days previously when, with ten days' rations they set out to negotiate an unconquered feature known as Low's Gully.

It had all begun as a noble enterprise; the brainchild of Lieutenant Colonel Neill, the darker of the pair, who dreamed of a successful, ground-breaking venture of derring-do to mark the birth of a new Corps to which the expedition members either directly or indirectly belonged. The hope was that the achievement would be to the Corps what the conquest of Everest had been to the Coronation of Queen Elizabeth II. Unfortunately, for reasons to be revealed, the exercise backfired badly. Instead of reputations being enhanced, they suffered from too much 'derring' and too little 'do'.

These five who found themselves in this serious, life-threatening predicament, were only half of those who had set out. A recurring theme of discussion among the two chess players was why the other, younger, fitter, more able five, who had gone on ahead, had apparently abandoned them to their fate. No less perplexing were the questions relating to their long-awaited rescue. Despite the by now regular sighting of helicopters 1,000ft above them, they were completely mystified as to why they remained undetected. But then, they did not fully comprehend the almost impossible position in which they had put themselves. This five-mile-long ravine was a place where angels would have feared to tread. There was, however, more to this débâcle than met the eye, and its revelation presents a fascinating cocktail of internal conflict, failure to heed advice, loss of communication and control, an element of misfortune and a mission rendered impossible by its unworkable team composition. Naturally, all stories must begin at the beginning. Strangely, in this particular case, the origins of this story of the Descent into Low's Gully lie in the middle of the nineteenth century.

Great Britain's connection with Borneo (Borneo is a corruption of the word 'Brunei') began at the end of July 1839 when James Brooke, an independent British imperialist from India, landed in the northern province of Sarawak to establish his own fiefdom. He found the weather on arrival to be somewhat typical: rain, thunder and lightning. Shortly after his arrival, James Brooke became involved in putting down a rebellion during a civil war. As a reward for re-establishing the status quo, the Borneans conferred upon him the title of White Rajah. Other than for a short period during the Second World War, Brooke and his descendants remained in Borneo in a position of authority for over a century.

The northern coast of Borneo lies just to the south of the typhoon zone, with Sabah in the top portion washed by the South China Sea to the west and the Sulu Sea and Celebes Sea to the east. Indeed, Sabah means 'below the wind'. It was for that reason Sabah was favoured for centuries by merchant sailors who benefited from its safe harbour trading area. Settlement at Kota (city) Kinabalu, so named in 1967, predates recorded history. Among its many former names is Api Api, meaning 'fire, fire' when, as a private port, its inhabitants frequently burnt the settlement down. Prior to Malaysia's independence, the port was called Jesselton. Lying as it does between Malaysia, Indonesia and the Philippines, Borneo was always likely to become a political football. Sabah has a central position in the middle of Australasia. Its capital, Kota Kinabalu, is 994 miles (1,600 km) from Singapore, 1,180 miles (1,900 km) from Kuala Lumpur and Hong Kong, 600 miles (965 km) from Manila and 1,490 miles (2,400 km) from Darwin.

In early times, the full range of natural resources contained within the inhospitable terrain of the world's third largest island could only be imagined. There were certainly oil and virgin rainforests of hardwood. It was considerations such as these which resulted in the British North Borneo Company being founded in 1881 to administer the territory. The capital of Sabah (it assumed the status of capital in 1946), Jesselton, took its name from the Company's Vice-Chairman, Sir Charles Jessel. On 9 January 1942, the Japanese invaded Sabah. During the period of Japanese occupation, the British name of Jesselton was dropped in favour of something with historical antecedents, Api. During the course of the war, Jesselton was virtually destroyed by allied bombing. Of the three buildings to survive, one was the Inland Revenue. At the end of hostilities the British North Borneo Company was patently unable to rebuild Sabah and, in 1945, it became a Crown Colony.

At the conclusion of the Second World War, the peoples of the larger, southern part of the island chose to join the fledgling state of Indonesia. The new state had been a by-product of the collapse of Dutch colonialism, and southern Borneo, renamed Kalimantan, became but one component in a new constellation of far-flung

Indonesian islands. The northern Borneo states of Brunei, Sabah and Sarawak, however, remained under British colonial administration. This served to deter the covetous aspirations of larger neighbouring states. In 1962 the Philippines made a move for Brunei and Sabah but were blocked by British military countermeasures.

In 1963 Sabah and Sarawak joined the Malaysian Federation, but not before a number of guarantees had been secured so that life could continue uninterrupted. In Sabah's case, there was a memorandum of 20 points drawn up to safeguard the interests of the 30 races who make up today's population of one and a half million. Unlike peninsular Malaysia, the majority of Sabahans are Christian. However, the oil-rich sultanate of Brunei resisted Kuala Lumpur's entreaties to join, and became independent in 1984. The idea of the creation of a Malaysian Federation incorporating northern Borneo appalled Indonesia's President Sukarno, who saw it as naked neo-colonialism. His newly-emergent country was riven by political tensions emanating both from a strong communist presence and from a strong military. Statesmen facing domestic difficulties very often embark upon a foreign adventure in order to strengthen their position and foster national cohesion. Sukarno's solution was to attack Malaysia. The period between September 1964 and August 1966 is known colloquially as the period of Confrontation. Without the steadfast support of British armed forces, the relatively new Malaysian army might well have been unable to prevent the over-running of North Borneo. The resultant impasse in the jungle did not provide Sukarno with his intended short, victorious war. Domestic public opinion hardened against him and he was forced to sue for peace and hand over political control to General Suharto early in 1967.

Hugh Low, the colonial treasurer of Labuan, comes to our attention the decade after Sir James Brooke's arrival in Sarawak. But for one event, he would have been but one of the numerous British colonial administrators whose remote, routine employment guaranteed that their names and reputations would not long survive their deaths. The resurrection and rehabilitation of Low, however, is coincidentally due to an event which occurred in 1994. The common denominator connecting two events almost one and a half centuries apart is the so-called haunted mountain of Borneo, Mount Kinabalu in Sabah. Mount Kinabalu had its origins one and a half million years ago when a massive granite rock which had been cooled and hardened began to rise and pierce the top crusts of softer rocks. It is therefore the youngest non-volcanic mountain in the world and is still growing by around three cm a year. The meaning of the word Kinabalu has been lost in history. The resultant attempts to unlock the mystery have included such incompatible names as the Chinese Widow and Solitary Father. What seems more likely is that it is derived from 'Aki Nabalu' which, in the Dusun language, means 'the revered place of the dead'.

The first recorded physical research of Mount Kinabalu occurred in 1844. Anchored off what is now called Kota Kinabalu, Captain Edward Belcher, Royal Navy, cast his eyes upon a huge, mountainous rampart of bare rock standing inland, proud of the jungle. The sheer size impressed him to such a degree that he took measurements of the highest visible point of the edifice from the untaxing environment of his own quarterdeck. It was not until 1910 that truly scientific measurements were taken of the mountain. The result, 13,455 ft (4,101 m), placed Mount Kinabalu as the highest mountain in South and South-East Asia between the Himalayas and New Guinea's Mount Wilhelmina. What Belcher was never to know was that Kinabalu is a mountain of two faces. He had looked upon the more kindly face of the two.

But long before Belcher, other voyagers had passed this way. The 14th-century Arab sailor, Ibn Batuta, left the first record of a 'great mountain of clouds' which he had observed in North Borneo. 'At the foot of the mountain,' he wrote, 'arise black clouds accompanied by winds which rise up the sea and wreck all that is found on that sea.' In 1521 Pigafeta, student of Magellan, visited the Sultan of Brunei. While he was amazed by the wealth and riches he saw around him, he was awestruck by the antics of the leaf insects he encountered in the rainforests. He was amazed that the trees 'were making leaves which, when they fall, are alive and walk'.

In 1851, Hugh Low was the first non-native to make an attempt to reach Mount Kinabalu's summit. This was a prodigious enterprise for just one European. It is self-evident, yet often forgotten, that there are two aspects to climbing mountains: the ascent and the descent. Once within the surrounding tree line, other real hazards presented themselves, among which were headhunters, uneven terrain, and dangerous creatures of the forest including pythons and king cobras. Low set out from his base camp on 4 March 1851 and reached what he believed to be the summit on 11 March 1851. He found the top to be a mix of ridge and plateau, hence there are a number of summits. The actual summit is called Low's Peak and although allegedly the easiest of a number of peaks to scale, Low did not attempt to do so. There were other matters on his mind.

Low's porters, drawn from the local Kadazan tribe, began to show signs of unease to such a disturbing degree that their flight from the place became a distinct possibility. They believed the mountain top to be the home of the spirits of their ancestors. According to folklore, when one died, his or her soul would mark out the territory of their resting place with marks known as *kokoliton.* These places were known only to the priestesses or *bobollan* and, in Low's and subsequent times, climbers had to make sacrifices to appease the spirits of the mountain. Gifts and sacrifices were in multiples of seven – seven was considered a lucky number. Among the items to appease the souls of the departed were white chickens, white feathers, rice, betel nuts, sireh leaves and tobacco. Low went through this ritual beside pools close to Panar Laban in order to guarantee the retention of the porters. Panar Laban is derived from the word *ponomonlob,* meaning sacrifice. The altimeter Low had specially brought to measure the height of the mountain was found to be inoperable. Faced with rising cloud, he had barely time to finish a bottle of Madeira, offer a loyal toast to the Queen and to distant friends, before commencing the descent. However, there was sufficient time to make one important discovery when he went out onto a narrow, six-inch ridge between two pinnacles:

> On placing my breast against it and looking over the ridge, I gazed into a circular amphitheatre eighty yards broad, the bottom of which from its great depth and my position overhanging it was undiscernible, though I imagine I could see down two thousand feet.

Low had discovered the mountain's awesome, hidden northern face. The Dusun knew of the Gully but would have nothing to do with it. It was not its formidable aspect that deterred them but the legend of a dragon living somewhere near the Gully's top. The story goes that, many years ago, a group of Chinese entered the Gully and stole the dragon's fire. The dragon's fury raged uncontrolled and it put a curse upon the Chinese people so that any drawn to the mountain would be destroyed.

The attraction of the mountain drew Low and his friend Spenser St John, British Consul in Brunei, to undertake another expedition in 1858. 'Early in April,' wrote St John,

> I went over from Brunei to Labuan to join him [Low]. We waited 'till the 15th for a vessel, which we expected would bring us a supply of shoes, but as it did not arrive we started. This was the cause of most of our mishaps.

Their impatience meant that they had to traverse the jungle, clamber over slippery rocks and through streams in common boots. Blisters were an inevitable result. They discarded their boots and made their way barefoot, but so badly damaged and septic had Low's feet become that he could not proceed further. St John left Low in the care of natives before making his own way up the mountain accompanied by local bearers. After three days, St John reached the spot where, seven years previously, Low had stood. He found the peak cold; in fact there had been a hoar frost. (A later Kinabalu explorer, John Whitehead, writing in 1893, registered his surprise at the superfluity of his tropical clothing. He found a jersey sometimes necessary and recorded how he had needed to sleep under blankets.) Although the nineteenth-century colonial administrators oversaw far-flung parishes they were, understandably, personally very close. Hugh Low was a friend of James Brooke, and Spencer St John was not only at one time Secretary to Brooke, but would later write his biography. Up at the summit, St John found Low's madeira bottle with a message inside. Overcome by curiosity, St John went forward to look over the northern face, and saw:

> A deep chasm, surrounded on three sides by precipices, so deep that the eye would not reach the bottom: but the twitter of innumerable swallows could be distinctly heard as they flew in flocks below.

There was no descending here. Unable to get the altimeter to function, St John retraced his steps, organised a stretcher party for Low, and together they left the mountain. Low's curiosity did not extend only to exploration for he was also a keen botanist. It is not just the gully that bears his name. A buttercup and pitcher plant (Nepenthes) are also named after him.

Low and St John made a subsequent attempt to climb the mountain and to collect botanical specimens. St John came within forty feet of climbing the peak named after him. There was no great following rush of climbers drawn to Mount Kinabalu. For example, in June 1925, when Major Charles Enriquez of the 2/20th Burma Rifles took the first proper military expedition to Kinabalu, he estimated that his was only the 25th group to tackle the mountain. In fact it was the 32nd to follow Low's conquest of 1851.

Enriquez selected to accompany him a man with much experience of expeditions, San Nan, and a Rifleman Bilu Gan, both Kachin hillmen from the north-east Burma frontier and both jungle experts. 'The wisdom of this selection,' he wrote, 'was at all the time evident on Kinabalu where San Nan's resource and energy in cold and rain were invaluable.' Enriquez had with him his Burmese Scout, Maung Ba Kye and a locally-engaged Dusun interpreter by the name of Paud. 'An ascent of Kinabalu,' he said, 'requires a good deal of preparation.'

Not all Enriquez's group found the climb to have been straightforward. The Scout, Maung Ba Kye 'had found the ascent most trying, and had therefore exerted the most pluck in accomplishing it.' Enriquez was surprised at what he found on the mountain top. It was:

> by no means as flat as one might suppose from certain distant aspects of it and this is soon self evident, for on crossing the plateau it is found to end abruptly in a horrid abyss – a sort of 'crater'; a veritable Devil's cauldron of incredible depth whose walls rise in sheer precipices of thousands of feet. As the outer aspect of Kinabalu is of perpendicular lines, so also is its interior.

It was, Enriquez concluded, a 'terrifying sight'.

A standard definition of 'gully' is 'a channel or small valley, especially one cut by heavy rainwater'. From the top of Kinabalu, Enriquez surveyed the dramatic northern side of the mountain, a fault system fashioned as it had been by heavy rain, ice and glaciers ripping away millions of tons of rock to scour out a 2,700 ft chasm.

> The central abyss at our feet, in the heart of the mountain, or at least part of it, seems to have been included in the rather feeble term 'Low's Gully' which St John gave to the ravine by which Low reached the gap between the two pinnacles and from which he looked down into the chasm below.* For the terrific chasm itself, the name Low's Rift, Low's Chasm or Low's Abyss would be more appropriate. One can well

---

*The Low's Gully originally described by St John is 'the perpendicular cleft between the Donkey's Ears Peak and Tunku Abdul Rahman's Peak and the ravine leading to it from the south'. D V Jenkins in *Kinabalu, Summit of Borneo,* A Sabah Society Monograph, 1978, p. 49.

> understand how the austere character of Kinabalu has impressed the simple minded Dusun who live at its feet. Here are all the stern realities of nature – stupendous chasms, sheer cliffs, raging cataracts and barren rock upraised hundreds of feet above the tree limit. It is only natural that its uncompromising aloofness should have suggested to the human mind an unconquerable remoteness such as that to which men's spirits retire after death.

Over an hour had passed as the awestruck climbers stood still to absorb the wonders they beheld. By virtue of not moving about, they soon became conscious of the intense cold. 'Ice has been reported', continued Enriquez,

> but we found none, perhaps on account of the recent rain. On our arrival at the top visibility was good ... and even as we watched (the) flecks grew and hid that fair landscape, so that in quite a few minutes we looked down upon a rising sea of clouds. Then just as suddenly, mists came bowling down from above. A wind moaned among the peaks; and from the abyss, white lines of wraiths came hurrying along ridges, as if the ghostly inhabitants of Kinabalu were impatient to resume their age long solitude.

Climbing Kinabalu today requires less energy and drama than that described by Enriquez half a century ago. The mountain is unique, as is recognised by its dominant position on Sabah's State flag. It is magnificent without being necessarily pleasing to the sight and it is also a shy mountain, often wreathed in cloud. Mount Kinabalu is the focal point in a National Park established in 1962 to conserve Sabah's natural heritage and covering an area of 288 square miles (745 sq km), approximately the same size as the island republic of Singapore. Thousands of visitors come to the Park each year to see its flora and fauna and to enjoy the temperate climate. Within the Park boundaries is one of the world's most unique ecological systems. There are 1,500 varieties of orchid, 25 species of rhododendron, Rafflesia (a parasitic plant named after Sir Thomas Raffles and with a fragrance of rotten meat which, with a diameter of up to three feet (one metre) is the world's largest flower), a wide selection of animal life, 300 species of birds, a multitude of reptiles and amphibians, and a whole host of insects – beetles, moths and butterflies. Many of the above varieties are endemic, found only on Mount Kinabalu and nowhere else in the world. The variation of altitude from 498 ft (152 metres) to 12,962 ft (3,952 metres) means that within this National

Park are specific plant zones ranging from alpine, through montane forest (where chestnut, oak and rhododendron are common) to the jungles of the lower reaches. The rains fall in Sabah during October to January but there are significant regional variations. The driest part of the year is between February and May, but the dryness is relative. An average day begins with a brilliantly clear morning followed by clouding and afternoon showers.

Visitors wishing to climb Mount Kinabalu can do so along the established, tourist mountain track. Climbing boots are recommended, as are waterproofs and warm clothing. There is no requirement for climbing *per se*, it being in effect a steep, uphill walk, well within the capability of most healthy and physically fit people. The climb was institutionalised in the 1980s with the introduction of a Climbathon during the months of September or October. The Climbathon is somewhat like a mini-marathon to the peak and back. The event attracts runners and the less ambitious from all over the world. The Gurkhas often feature among the prizes. Their own Khud* race is an important event in their own military sporting calendar. Whereas the average tourist allows two days to go up and back, the best runners can do the circuit in under two and a quarter hours. The two-day hike for ordinary mortals, from Park Headquarters to the summit and back, includes an overnight stay in a hut on the mountain – either the Panar Laban Huts (3,344 m) or the Sayat-Sayat Hut (3,800 m). These huts are all self-contained, being equipped with bunk beds and cooking facilities. Use of the Sayat-Sayat Hut is not encouraged because of complications with sanitation. For the climber, as opposed to the trekker, there are many climbs of varying degrees of difficulty, many yet to be recorded and registered.

The Park authorities retain tight control over climbers on the mountain. For example, visitors are obliged to use an authorised guide. There are porters available for hire to carry their gear. Day One of the tourists' climb ends in one of the mountain huts. In order to reach the summit by dawn, Reveille is usually at 3am. The last part of the climb is strenuous. With their way illuminated by the penlights of a million stars, the climbers haul themselves upward, as though on a funicular railway, up a tethered ropeway, progressing slowly, as if

*From the verb *khudnu*, to climb.

cog by cog, along the slippery path. On occasion, the wind makes its unwelcome contribution to the enthusiasts' burden, in the same way as the early morning cold and the by now enervating influence of altitude sickness. But once there, on the summit, there is for most an overwhelming sense of achievement and the anticipation of witnessing the unfolding of one of the world's most magnificent spectacles. Once released, the bright rays of the morning sun awaken and reveal the depth and breadth of the countryside below. On a really clear day the island of Banggi can be seen to the north and the vast, lower expanse of lesser mountains running up the west coast of Borneo. Also to the north there is, of course, Low's Gully.

It is natural, with so many thousands of people climbing Mount Kinabalu each year and returning by the same route, that there would inevitably be those who pondered the challenge of descending the mountain via Low's Gully. It is a prospect that has been nibbled at over the recent past. In fact an earlier British Army expedition attempted to descend and ascend Low's Gully with the aim of making rendezvous somewhere in the middle. It failed. While the descent of Low's Gully is undoubtedly achievable by well-trained and well-equipped teams, the ascent represents a much higher degree of difficulty.

In 1988, Robert New, a Sabah businessman with climbing experience in the French and Swiss Alps, Norway and Uganda, teamed up with an alpinist of considerable repute, Steve Pinfield, to attempt the descent into Low's Gully. Pinfield had been asked by the Sabah Society to supply them with photographs of his next descent into Low's Gully and this was the reason for the 1988 expedition. On an earlier trip, Pinfield had taken two Swiss climbers some way down the Gully but had not brought back pictures. Both New and Pinfield had considerable experience of the conventional climbs in and around Mount Kinabalu. Five years earlier, New had climbed to the summit with his 13-month-old son on his back. For him and Pinfield, therefore, the summit had long since lost its magic.

After their first exploration in 1988, they were coming out of the Gully using jumars* when it began to rain. The bottom of Low's Gully was obviously no place to be when the rain came off the mountain.

---

*A jumar is a ratchet device attached to a rope which has a loop below it in which the climber's foot is placed. Operated in pairs, by hand, they are moved up a rope, allowing the climber to ascend the rope step by step.

The narrowing that occurs lower down could leave people stranded between the rock face and the river – a desperate situation to be in. They had only a short retreat to beat but the rain left a deep impression on them. The danger had served only to whet their appetites. They planned another expedition down the Gully and, once at the bottom, rather than climb back with the use of ratchets attached to their ropes, intended to follow the rocky stream bed to the Panataran River. The pair set off on this expedition in 1990. Whilst in the process of descending a steep slab, Steve Pinfield lost his footing and slid towards the lip of a chasm. He saved his life by grabbing and holding on to some vegetation, but the fall had served to dislocate his shoulder and the quest had to be aborted. The pair's decision not to be beaten was immediate; so much so that they squirrelled away the equipment they had with them under House Boulder. They returned to their respective homes with the hope of re-addressing Low's Gully in the drier period of April 1991.

This time the pair spent the first night at 13,000 ft in the Sayat-Sayat Hut (the local name for the bushy Leptospermum plant commonly found in the area). Their outline plan was to spend four days in the Gully. They believed speed to be of the essence so as to minimise the risk of wet weather and to that end they travelled light, carrying no more than 40 lb/18 kg in their rucksacks. As before, they climbed above Sayat-Sayat Hut to the Easy Valley col* between Tunku Abdul Rahman Peak and King Edward Peak, and then descended Easy Valley. Easy Valley lies beneath the vertical rock faces of King George Peak and descends down ever steeper rock slabs into Low's Gully itself. New and Pinfield located the boulder where they had left their equipment the previous year and stopped there for lunch. Retrieving what they wanted, they resumed their approach, following a steep, vegetated stream bed to a point where the stream dives sheer over a lip and abseiling is necessary. The point of no return is reached when the ropes used to abseil are recovered because there is then no way back up. 'This was the turning point,' said New,

> It was our most committing moment because once we had pulled our abseil ropes down, we were committed to getting off the mountain by a route no one has ever used before.

---

*A col is a strip of land or a ridge connecting two peaks.

By evening they were in the bottom of the Gully and camped on a flat rock in the dry river bed. So committed were they to travelling light that every single item was given careful consideration. They took only essentials, even limiting themselves to two 50 m (164 ft) ropes. During the 1960s Borneo campaign, SAS soldiers operating in the jungle had also pursued the philosophy of going light, to the degree that one spoon sufficed for every member in a patrol. New and Pinfield bought themselves only six days' rations. Sleeping bags had been among the first items to be rejected. Their first night out on the mountain turned out to be a cold night.

On the second day they continued their way down into the Gully which, by good fortune, contained only partial stretches of retained water. The irregular water obstacles, sometimes narrow, sometimes broad, presented no immediate problems when compared with the enormous boulders along their way, interspersed with patchy jungle. The water-washed boulders stood out prominently along the steep watercourse. The ten feet boulders could be slid down but the fifteen feet boulders were something of a different order – they had to be bypassed. The problem with very large boulders was not only the difficulty in establishing abseil points but also the friction which prevented recovery of the rope. In such circumstances they would cut off into the jungle along the side of the river. It was not primary jungle but very high, thick shrubbery – something which slowed down the progress of the two men carrying packs and swinging machetes. Along the river they encountered sheer rock faces to either side, but it was unusual to find such walls opposite one another. Then came another steep drop which, once again, for the second and last time required the two 50 m ropes to be unrolled, the karabiners clipped on at waist level, the positioning of bodies at right angles to the cliff face, the first exhilarating leap outward, away from the rock, and then downward by leaps and bounds. Progress continued to be made until 4pm, when they were confronted by a real physical teaser. In front of them the Gully narrowed to a steep-sided gorge, from which the stream fell twenty feet into a small lake. There was no possible purchase on the rock faces rising vertically several hundred feet from both sides of the water along which they could negotiate their way downward. A further complication was that they could also see, beyond the immediate obstacle, a similar problem further down the Gully. It was a good place, therefore, to break for the night and to pause for thought.

In the morning of their third day they surveyed the situation in front of them, but this only served to confirm what they had pondered during the night. Not only were they not equipped to swim the pools but they did not have with them the specialist equipment needed to traverse the gorge. Of the two sides, the right hand side appeared the less daunting, so they set out along a narrow ledge in the hope of moving up and over into another valley. Before long their ledge petered out and they were forced to drop down onto a lower ledge, but that only took them into thick shrubbery. There was no way through. They returned to the camp site of the night before to reflect upon their situation. Both climbers had been used to technically difficult routes on numerous mountains throughout the world. However, all these routes had been previously well documented. There were no surprises to detract from the function of climbing. In the Gully, however, New and Pinfield had launched themselves into the unknown.

Their minds made up, they retraced their steps a short distance, climbing out of the Gully through steep, rattan-covered slopes. After a couple of hours they came to a ridge from where they decided to resume their descent down a not unreasonable slope. After approximately 1,500 ft they came again to a point where the ground dropped vertically in front of them. From here they could see that if they had continued down along the watercourse they would have had to face a series of descending obstacles comprising terraces of pools. But there was an unforeseen hazard in moving away from the water sources. They had brought no water bottles for, at the time, it seemed self-evident that they would never be far removed from a river bed. Robert New had become badly dehydrated and consequently acutely depressed that they would never find their way out of the Gully. Steve Pinfield encouraged him on as, once again, they climbed upward to find a way out of their predicament. By this time Robert New was exhausted, unable to find enough saliva even to dilute a piece of chocolate stuck in his throat:

> I've felt tired in previous mountaineering expeditions elsewhere but never as exhausted as on the third day in trying to come out of the gully. Whether it has anything to do with age I don't know. But we were lugging quite heavy packs over some of the steepest terrain and under great psychological pressure to make it, especially me with a wife and two kids waiting at home.

They got to the top of a sharp ridge and rested, and Pinfield commented that they seemed to have stumbled onto a path. He got up to look around and investigate what he at first believed to be an animal trail. However, a discarded toffee paper found on the ground meant that this was a track which had been created by men, possibly attempting to climb up to North Peak. Their hopes soared, but as they continued their descent the terrain did not become any more friendly. Tarzan-like, they climbed under overhanging roots. Then, shortly, they came to a tree with 'February 1990' carved upon it. They guessed that the mark had been left by a British Army Royal Engineers expedition attempting to climb Kinabalu East via the north ridge. They continued down the very steep trail, into another valley in which flowed a stream, a tributary of the Panataran. Thankfully they rested, taking their first real drink of the cool water since their overnight stop on Day Three.

The next morning, the fifth day, they followed the stream until they came to a hunter's camp site. From here there was a clear trail which took them away from the river, over a series of ridges, and into another hunters' camp. Here they spent the night before reaching Melangkap Kappa on the sixth and final day. Unfortunately for them it was a public holiday and therefore there was no transport. 'How far to the nearest road?', they asked. 'Three miles,' came the reply. After three miles they asked a different person. 'How far to the nearest road?' 'Three miles.' Three miles later the process was repeated. Eventually they hit the road and got a lift back to Kota Belud.

New and Pinfield had made the first successful descent from Kinabalu to the bottom via the upper section of Low's Gully, yet they had not done so along the full length of the Gully. The array of pools squeezed between sheer cliffs had forced them off course, away to the east. New admitted that 'there is still a section of about half a mile from there to the main Panataran River that has not been traversed yet and can still be a challenge for someone.' He told the press that if he was to make the attempt again he would know what he was up against and be better prepared to negotiate the pools. 'But then,' he paused, 'I have a family to think about and I am not quite as young (44) as I used to be.' Neither he nor Steve Pinfield made another attempt to descend the length of Low's Gully.

In November 1992, eighteen months after his attempt to conquer Low's Gully, Robert New had a significant interview with James Sarda, feature writer for the local *Daily Express* newspaper. He said that he had not been a regular taker of exercise but argued that besides physical strength, there was a requirement for a great deal of stamina. 'It has more to do with having a great sense of knowing what you are doing,' he explained, 'and making the right decisions as you are going along than actually being fit, because you're not going fast or racing against time.' He commented upon the pair's extreme good fortune that it had not rained at all, particularly when they were in the Gully:

> It would be foolhardy to attempt it during bad weather as waterfalls can develop within minutes of a rainfall. And since the top is bare rock with nothing to slow it, the water will run off the steep sides very quickly and cascade dramatically. It would have been the most dangerous place to be under those circumstances.

Rescue would have been difficult if not out of the question. A key factor in attempting to conquer Low's Gully in May was the weather. Rain was possible at any time, but May usually provided the best promise of prolonged dry spells. But there was to be no hanging around: the aim was to get in and get out as quickly as possible before it started to rain:

> The Parks knew we were doing the expedition. We gave them a date when we thought we would come out. But, frankly, what could they do even if we didn't show up by then? They wouldn't know exactly where we were. Even if they could locate us they would not be able to get at us because it is virtually impossible to get a helicopter in there.

It was this consideration which had the greatest impact upon New, the 'great sense of isolation and helplessness in the face of such a dramatic landscape'. He admitted:

> It had a very powerful effect on me, not a matter of being frightened, but you feel loneliness tremendously in such a situation. When we got to the army camp site (the tree upon which 'February 1990' had been carved) we experienced a great sense of relief, of having made it and an underlying sense of achieving what we had set out to do.

This elation compared with the earlier depression emphasised how essential it was that the overwhelming sense of despair had to be gripped. The pair's culminating moment of crisis came when they found their way effectively blocked by the series of pools, New's Pools, and no apparent escape. 'We knew then that we would have to cope with this. We did not know at that stage how we were going to deal with it and we were worried.' Well before the expedition had begun, there were siren voices advising them not to go, not to pry into the secrets of the haunted mountain of Borneo. 'They felt we might have desecrated a sacred place,' explained New,

> I don't think Low's Gully has any spiritual significance. But some people feel there are places you should leave to nature. It was a particular feature of the mountain that has intrigued me and I really wanted to go down there and see what it was like.

As we shall see, this interest was by no means unique. The importance of the New and Pinfield expedition was that it set a standard by which Neill's group and those to follow would measure their own progress down the Gully. It seems that aspiring expedition leaders should ask themselves initially why the Gully had remained unconquered, and set the answering of that key question as their planning start point.

2
Preparations

Robert Neill was born in November 1947. In December 1968, following officer training, he joined the Glosters, an infantry regiment. After somewhat less than four years as an infanteer, with his hearing impaired by gunfire, he transferred to Supply. In 1980, he was in Hong Kong as a junior major, employed in the Supply Depot. He had already developed an interest in adventurous pursuits and it was here in Hong Kong that he became acquainted with Kinabalu. Aged 33, he was a fit man with a lot of energy and was a competent organiser. He put these skills together to design and lead adventurous training exercises for the British and Chinese members of the Hong Kong Composite Ordnance Depot. The first of these, in March 1981, Exercise Jungle Heights 1, took his team up the conventional tourist track of Kinabalu and included some limited exploration of the summit. It was whilst there that Neill first looked down into the abyss of Low's Gully. The next exercise in the series was held in Western Malaysia, but in 1982 Exercise Jungle Heights 3 returned to Kinabalu, Eastern Malaysia.

In 1982, the then Major Neill led an adventure training exercise, Jungle Heights 3, formed from nine volunteers of the Composite Ordnance Depot, Hong Kong, back to Kinabalu. The team comprised the deputy, Warrant Officer Class I Ronald Foster, then aged 42, four British non-commissioned officers and three locally employed Chinese soldiers. The exercise, from 17 November to 1 December 1982, had as its aim the climbing of Mount Kinabalu from the north, from the area of Kampong Melangkap, along the Panataran River and up Low's Gully to the summit. Neill had explored the summit during Jungle Heights 1 and found a route from the top of Low's Gully. It was on the basis of this that he made the deduction that: 'providing the Panataran River could be followed upstream until it reached the gully, the summit could be safely reached.' What was not known, he added, was 'the nature of the river, the jungle bordering it or the lower reaches of the gully'. What Neill was in effect saying was that, other than what he could see from around the summit, he had no idea what he was letting himself in for. But then it is certainly possible to fail to achieve an adventurous training mission, yet still satisfy the adventurous training criteria of benefiting leadership, training and morale. It comes back to the aim: is it to provide adventure and experience to novices, or is it an attempt to do something really difficult, requiring peak fitness and ability standards? Such aims seem to be mutually exclusive.

Neill took his 1982 expedition to Mount Kinabalu at what was almost the wettest period of the year. His unit programme meant that this was the only time of the year the expedition could be launched, but what was perhaps more disagreeable was the fact that the Royal Brunei Airline chartered seats for the Hong Kong–Brunei flight were at that time available only once a fortnight. Moreover, the flights from Brunei to Kota Kinabalu did not fit the exercise timetable, which meant that the team had to travel from Brunei to Sabah by sea and over land. The effect of all these combined factors on the time and space appreciation was that only seven days could be spared for the trekking part and five days reserved for movement.

The advantage Jungle Heights 3 had over what was to follow was the fact that all the volunteers came from the same unit, which assisted team compatibility and meant that command and control considerations were unlikely to give rise to friction. There was also an organised group fitness training schedule which commenced on 17 September 1982. Sessions such as this derive additional benefit from the opportunity to improve team familiarisation with one another and among pairs who would bivouac together and share loads. The Chinese team members were assimilated into the group. Neill regarded the weight of packs to be critical. The optimum weight to carry equipment and seven days' rations was 50 lb (22 kg), for up to eight hours and 20 km (12½ miles) a day over a range of plus or minus 1,000 m (3,280 ft).

On the first two days of their expedition the team had walked seven miles, to a height of approximately 2,000 ft. The river, which at the outset had been found to be clear, shallow and wide, had now become a monster, blocked by massive boulders and floored with slippery rocks, with torrents forging their paths through deep rapids.

The rain fell as usual in the afternoon. There was now no question of being able to follow the watercourse any further, which meant that Day 3 would begin with an assault on the jungle to cut a path parallel to the river. They found the steeply rising terrain to be covered with a scree of stones which showered downhill upon those following behind. The undergrowth proved to be unyielding, and soon hands had sacrificed much of their skin. The ground began to fall away, necessitating the use of ropes, which in turn worsened the state of the men's hands. Ants then came in to attack, followed by small wasps which had painful stings. Then, on top of all this, it rained very heavily. In a short period of time the water level in the river had risen by three feet, thus making it effectively an uncrossable obstacle. In one day, the team had covered a matter of a few hundred yards. Major Neill and Warrant Officer Foster went forward to reconnoitre a path which hopefully would take them out of their predicament. Their post-exercise report recorded that from the ridge overlooking the river they had seen the torrent below, very narrow and in spate, flowing along with a tremendous force and speed. Worse still, the cliffs fell sheer into the river on both sides for as far as they could see.

The impossibility of the mission they had set themselves was now self-evident. They had used almost half their time and rations to climb up the easiest seven miles to a height of only 2,000 ft (610 m). The next seven miles required a climb of 10,000 ft (3,049 m). To have pressed on, with the river in its swollen condition, would have been an unacceptable risk to life and limb. The steep cliff faces gave rise to special concern for, if caught between them by a flash flood, there would be no escape. The option of moving parallel to the river, through the jungle, proved to be nugatory. Neill decided to abort the expedition then and there and to seek, by way of solace, a return to the summit before having to begin the journey to take them back to Hong Kong. The expedition had comprehensively failed to even approach the successful conclusion of its mission. The reasons Neill gave were the flooded Panataran River, the difficult nature of the river bed and the jungle alongside it, and what he described as the time/distance/rations factor. Any successful conquest of Low's Gully from this direction, therefore, would have to avoid the consequences of flooding, with the attendant complications affecting the option of going along the watercourse and the parallel undergrowth, and making some sensible time and space appreciation upon which conclusions as to food and equipment requirements could be made.

The reflections as to how best to tackle Low's Gully in the future still banked on the northern approach. Moreover they had accepted the time constraints imposed by a twice-weekly air service. There is an ingrained acceptance of the limitations imposed by an inflexible air transport regime. The need for more time was self-evident, and therefore there had to be an increase in the amount of food to be carried. One proposed answer was to use half the team as food mules or porters to accompany the other half of the team two to three days up river and, after replenishing their stocks of rations, to withdraw and meet the climbers at the top of Low's Gully where a further replenishment could be effected. (It would transpire that on Exercise Gulley Heights, each man carried ten days' food and, although porters were available, they were not hired.)

A year later, in August 1983, another attempt was made on Low's Gully during Exercise Jungle Heights 4. The expedition, of which Foster was a member, divided into two, half coming along the Panataran River and the other half descending from the peak. It was during the course of this expedition that a serious misappreciation was made. Whilst in the process of converging, both teams had mountains between them and were unable to use the radios they had with them to make contact. The conclusion was reached that radios would not work in the Gully, even though on Gulley Heights the nature and conduct of the exercise was entirely different. On Exercise Gulley Heights the team did not approach from different directions but followed the same route down, where line of sight did prove possible. It also seems highly possible that if the groups which became separated had had radios, then the team leader might have regained control of his expedition. 'Radios' fall into two quite specific groups: those used by an expedition to talk to other parties and those to be used for communication with the group. Neill had neither.

In May–June 1988 a further expedition in which Foster was a team member, Kinabalu Triangle, was sponsored by the 17/21 Lancers. The aim of Kinabalu Triangle had been to follow the Panataran River the nine miles (14 km) through the jungle between the end of the track at Kampong Melankap to Low's Gully. The organisers had taken 'particular care' that the expedition coincided with the dry season so that the low water level in the river would facilitate their speedy passage along it. Once at the mouth of Low's Gully, they would decide whether it was technically feasible to climb Low's Peak from an approach up through Low's Gully. The Lancers' team was based in Münster, Germany, whereas the then Captain Foster, now commissioned in the Territorial Army, was in England. The Lancers' end of expedition report stated that Kinabalu Triangle had been 'the brainchild of Captain Foster who was also the driving force'. However, planning was severely circumscribed because the practical, first-hand experience upon which they so depended (Foster's) was initially only transmitted 'occasionally by telephone'. This fact had ramifications, with team training affected not only by the Regiment's busy schedule but also due to 'a lack of knowledge of what was going to be confronted'.

The progress of the Lancers' 1988 expedition is worthy of study. Although they had taken particular care to arrive in Sabah during the dry season, regional variations meant that they worked in a perpetual monsoon. This was May, *a month which falls within the dry season.* The Panataran River was so swollen and fast flowing that they were unable to make the intended rapid progress along it and the danger of flash floods could not be discounted. All eight of the team members set out together along the river. Not only were they slowed down by the flow of the river but their heavily laden bergen rucksacks, once immersed in water, became heavier still. Their day of decision came on Day 6, a day on which Foster cut his hand on a submerged rock. It was agreed that 'the size of the expedition had been a contributory factor to the previous day's slow progress'. Accordingly, a decision was taken to divide the group into two four-men teams. Half were to continue while the other half, which included Foster, after treatment had been given to his hand, were to retrace their tracks and go via Park Headquarters up the tourist track to the top of Mount Kinabalu. At the summit, this group intended to abseil down into Easy Valley to explore possible routes in and out of Low's Gully. Once at the summit, Foster's group divided into pairs. They made limited progress before giving up in the face of the continuing storm which threatened to wash them off the mountain. Eventually, both groups of four withdrew, not having come close to completing their missions.

Three factors combined to frustrate this expedition. Firstly, the monsoon weather occurring in the 'dry season' had its own wrecking influences. Sabah's weather is notoriously unpredictable. Secondly, the eight-men team was deemed to have been too large to maintain the intended schedule. Thirdly, the bergen rucksacks loaded with essential food and equipment to cope with climbing in and out of the river, through jungle and over slippery rocks, were too heavy. When they became wet they became an added burden.

In 1990, ten years after the first, limited expedition to Kinabalu, Neill and Foster met again. They talked of old times and discovered that their mutual desire to conquer Low's Gully was undiminished. They made an outline plan to launch yet another, probably the final, foray onto Borneo's haunted mountain. The detailed planning was put on the 'back burner' due to the intervention of the Gulf conflict. Then, in 1993, Foster holidayed in Kota Kinabalu. Whilst in Sabah, Foster met Robert New and obtained copies of the account of New's expedition which had appeared in the local *Daily Express*, 29 November 1992 and 6 December 1992.

Foster's meeting with New was of considerable importance. Here was Foster who, by his own admission, had had a career of 'formidable physical activity'. He met the tall, slim, self-deprecating New, and it does seem that Foster underrated him. Foster certainly did not come away with a clear impression as to the difficulties involved in descending into Low's Gully. The fact that neither Pinfield nor New had taken water bottles with them on their expedition was viewed as an elementary and dangerous mistake and served to reinforce the already erroneous underestimation of New and Pinfield. In *SOS*, Foster was to record that New was not averse to making another attempt. This strangely contradicts what Foster wrote in a letter to Neill, when he specifically mentions New's reluctance to embark upon another venture down Low's Gully. It also ran entirely contrary to what New had told Sarda. He did indeed say that if he was to make another attempt he would be better prepared, but he put in an important caveat: '. . . but then, I have a family to think about and I am not quite as young as I used to be.' Nevertheless, he had been two years younger than Neill and ten years younger than Foster.

Neill examined the details of New's expedition very carefully, mindful all the time that New was 'by no means an Olympic athlete'. As a result of misreading New and Sarda's article, Neill gravely underestimated the difficulties involved in tackling Low's Gully. Had he been fully acquainted with the facts, he would possibly have not taken the team that he did. He believed he could lead a new expedition down into Low's Gully, retracing New's route as far as New's Pools. From the evidence before him, Neill concluded that the New–Pinfield attempt had failed because they had travelled too light, neglecting to take with them sufficient food and equipment. He reasoned that a better-equipped team would be in a more favourable position to explore down the Gully, beyond where New and Pinfield aborted their attempt. If he was wrong, then the option of taking the pair's escape route would still be available.

Having therefore satisfied himself as to the proposed exercise's feasibility, Neill set about the process of making the necessary application for authority to proceed from the Directorate of Army Training. The pair were confident that their application would succeed for, as they said in their book, their 'own knowledge of Kinabalu was so extensive'.

In reality, Neill's and Foster's knowledge of Kinabalu was not as extensive as they imagined; neither had been in Low's Gully proper. A crucial, major problem arose from their confused thinking as to the relevance of abseiling. They did observe that New and Pinfield, who had gone down in the dry, had only taken two 50 m ropes, from which they concluded that abseiling would not be 'a significant factor' of their expedition. But the lightly-laden New and Pinfield were high-grade mountaineers who could scramble down water courses which heavily-laden novices would have to negotiate by rope. Apparently this difference had not registered with Neill and Foster. Otherwise, in a situation where time and space were ultra-critical, they would not have taken novices with them. And yet the contradictions continue. Having admitted in their book that abseiling had not been a 'significant factor', they write of needing their ropes 'again and again', and even say that their expedition was interested 'principally in abseiling rather than climbing'.

Adventurous Training has an important, incontrovertible niche in an army's overall training package. During the training year 1993–94, 35% of the United Kingdom's Field Army took part in some form of adventurous training. The litmus test as to whether such an exercise has been of benefit to the Service and to the individuals is to determine whether *leadership* skills have been enhanced, the *training* has been beneficial and *morale* has been strengthened. 'There is little need to justify the philosophy of Adventurous Training,' stated a British Army policy document.

> A good soldier needs mental and moral self-discipline as well as physical strength and endurance; he needs to be accustomed to danger, hardship and challenge and these are not easy to provide

> within the constraints of normal peace-time training. The basic skills and craft required during training in challenging pursuits in a natural environment enormously enhance the complementary military skills essential in a professional soldier. These skills, which are basically those of the traditional countryman, are less and less inherent in the young men of today brought up in an ever-increasing urban environment. Additionally, Adventurous Training strengthens self-confidence, forces those participating to accept responsibility and to make decisions; it is thus invaluable in the development and training of potential leaders. The aim of Adventurous Training is to provide these opportunities through participation in challenge pursuits and expeditions, and those participating are to be considered as on duty.

The British soldier has long been associated with adventure and exploration; a fact which can be emphasised by a recruiting machine at a time when opportunities for overseas posting and travel have declined significantly. Captain Oates, who was a member of Scott's fateful expedition, had been a cavalry officer; British soldiers were on top of Everest long before it became a routine occurrence; and the Royal Engineer John Blashford Snell's association with Operation Raleigh serves to emphasise the military's pre-eminence in this field. Adventurous Training is the greenhouse for the more substantial, properly organised and properly funded expedition. It is essential that the difference between the two is fully understood. The levels of training and skills required are of a different order. There is much less public reaction if a soldier is killed or injured on a properly constituted Army or Joint Services expedition than in an adventurous training pursuit. The stringent rules under which Adventurous Training is conducted are often criticised for stifling adventure. The problem has been that after each adventurous training mishap, a Board of Inquiry is formed and will recommend the imposition of added safeguards which merely accumulate to contradict the aim of the activity; that is, one 'requiring participation in challenging pursuits which contain a risk to life and limb'. It is therefore a difficult area in which to draw the line when seeking to provide the challenges of war at a time of peace.

An adventure training exercise will usually originate as a challenge the organiser himself will want to address. In order for the Service to give him the time off and the financial support, he has to form his team comprising varying ranks and mixed abilities. The analogy used to reflect the composition of the team is that of a 'pyramid'. The selection of novices and junior ranks is encouraged and the officer to junior rank ratio is not permitted to exceed 50:50. Commanding officers have to declare at the time of their annual inspection the extent of adventurous training conducted in their unit during the year and have to maintain a specified cadre of qualified adventurous training personnel. Commanders like to see their men getting away as much as the men enjoy a break from the monotony of routine. Adventurous Training is therefore a happy marriage of mutual convenience. Yet there are three residual problem areas. Very often there are insufficient instructors with the requisite qualifications; secondly, at a time when the army is overstretched, there is often a shortage of time for relevant training; and thirdly, there is the matter of funding.

Organisers are frequently left to find qualified personnel outside their own unit. There is not an inexhaustible number, and their own commanding officers, understandably, prefer these men to support their own adventurous training programme rather than someone else's. Where latitude does exist, the qualified people will often pick and choose, preferring those exercises which, for them, are the most challenging and invariably held in interesting foreign countries. The time-shortage is best circumvented in formed units which have the benefit of living in one barracks. The 17/21 Lancers are a good example. In that manner, evenings and weekends can be devoted to skills, stamina and fitness training. In addition, the nature of an integral regiment means that little time has to be spent on team-bonding. Understandably, where these circumstances do not exist, where individuals are drawn from different regiments in different regions, special attention has to be given to finding time for individual and compatibility training of the team.

There are grants available for Adventurous Training, but it is an accepted principle of this activity that there has to be a personal contribution. In the case of small expeditions, the individual is expected to subscribe one third of the total cost of the expedition, while for larger exercises the rate is not less than one quarter of the member's daily pay for the duration of the exercise. The Services are well paid, but are notoriously reluctant to put their hands in their pockets, particularly for an activity that fulfils an accepted training function. Regiments are not unused to subsidising the junior members, but financial stringency does often have an all-pervading influence upon the course and achievement of the exercise. There is an over-dependence upon obtaining free seats on Service aircraft, which in turn has an unsatisfactory influence upon the planning and the conduct of exercises.

By 1994 Neill, now a lieutenant colonel, was in Eastern District Headquarters, York. He was obliged to clear his plan with his commanding officer. His commanding officer's declared responsibilities were but another litany of requirements which, if all were undertaken, would bring effective work to a close. Army regulations require first and foremost that:

> the person responsible for the conduct and safety of an expedition should have well developed qualities of leadership, and be competent to lead his party in an emergency.

The commanding officer's role is to ensure that the leader's personal qualities, training and experience meet those criteria. In coming to his decision, the commanding officer is given four sets of factors to consider: firstly, the age, experience and physical fitness of the party members; secondly, the objective hazards, for example the height, steepness and remoteness of the expedition area and whether or not the expedition leader is familiar with it; thirdly, the time of the year and probable weather conditions; and lastly, clothing and equipment available. The principal problem was that although Lieutenant Colonel Neill's commanding officer was in effect *his* commanding officer, he was not commanding officer of the team members selected by Neill.

Neill's team selection was influenced by a rationalisation which had just occurred within the British Army. This was essentially the reintegration of the transportation and supply functions; yet, as is so often the case when a committee is set the task of designing a horse, it presents a camel. The opportunity to tidy up the army proved irresistible as not only were transportation and supply put into the melting pot to form a new Corps, but also tossed in were Postal Services, Pioneers and the Army Catering Corps. In the even-handed approach to try to be all things to all men and to reconcile all interests, the traditions or habits of the original constituent parts were selectively picked over to be incorporated into the new Corps. Named the Royal Logistic Corps, or RLC for short, and formed on 5 April 1993, it comprised 14 per cent of the British Army's strength and, for that reason, RLC was translated by wags into the 'Really Large Corps'. The Army Catering Corps' contribution to the RLC was to bequeath its motto, undoubtedly one that should have been buried deep during the course of amalgamation. But it was not to be, and the RLC was born with the Cooks' old motto, with its multiple meanings, 'We Sustain'. In view of what was to happen, the motto proved to be highly appropriate.

Neill and Foster took New's and Pinfield's expedition as the benchmark from which to determine how long they should allow for their expedition proper. They still maintained this serious underestimation of New's and Pinfield's ability. The civilians had undertaken their partial conquest in six days. Neill and Foster assessed that they were unlikely to do it in under six days, particularly since they had 'no intention of being forced out of the Gully like New'. They added a fudge factor of four days and determined that they could therefore defeat the Gully in ten days.

Neill and Foster had decided that the team should comprise a maximum of ten men of mixed abilities drawn from their new Corps, both the regular and territorial components. An even number is important so that pairs can look after one another and carry collective items. Later, having established a ceiling of five pairs, Neill and Foster attempted to co-opt New onto their expedition, without success. Neill was also particularly keen to continue the precedent he had established when serving in Hong Kong, by including three Chinese soldiers serving with the RLC. One essential task was to ensure that within the team there existed the mandatory qualifications for the type of Adventurous Training he proposed to conduct on Mount Kinabalu. This was essentially trekking but would also involve rock climbing and abseiling. Since Low's Peak was below the snow line, the qualification requirement was not as stringent as it might otherwise have been.

The minimum qualifications for the leader of the expedition to Kinabalu were either the Joint Service Mountaineering Expedition Leader (Summer) or the Mountain Leadership Certificate (Summer). Both qualifications permit the leader to take parties of up to six novices and eight seasoned mountaineers in mountainous country but below the snow line, worldwide. Neill holds the Mountain Leadership Certificate, which he had been awarded in Norway almost twenty years earlier. Another member of the team, Lance Corporal Shearer, held the other qualification, Joint Service Mountaineering Expedition Leader, which covers the trekking phase. Neill recruited Lance Corporal Mayfield to oversee the climbing aspects of the expedition. He was a Joint Service Rock Climbing Instructor, a qualification of considerable weight. Mayfield was in the same league as Pinfield. He was supported by four members of the group who had qualified at the United Kingdom Land Forces School of Adventurous Training as Top Roping and Abseiling Instructors in November 1993. Not one of the team had jungle survival expertise. Although not required by regulations, it was nevertheless a curious oversight.

The team was selected gradually between July 1993 and January 1994. Major Ron Foster (54) became Robert Neill's (46) deputy leader. Sergeant Bob Mann (37), a territorial, and Lance Corporal Richard Mayfield (25), also a soldier, were selected from 3 Commando Brigade, where both were logisticians. Corporal Hugh Brittan (24), formerly of the Parachute Brigade, and Lance Corporals Peter Shearer (26) and Steve Page (26), volunteered and were accepted in November 1993. From the available evidence, soldiers cite one reason above all others for volunteering for adventurous training exercises, and that is the *challenge* the exercise poses. An Australian survey of Australian adventure training, published in 1987, showed that 91 per cent of those given the opportunity to join adventurous activity accepted it. Of these, 92 per cent enjoyed what they did, 5 per cent did not enjoy themselves, and 3 per cent had mixed reactions.

The fact that Brittan and Page were colleagues and Shearer was an outsider had implications during the latter phases of the expedition. Shearer had been a supply operator working with the Royal Engineers near Cambridge. Brittan and Page were the only two transport representatives in the supply-heavy team. It was Page who was originally confirmed as having a place on the expedition while Brittan joined through default. Both soldiers were members of the transport corps' Mobile Display Team, a recruiting venture aimed at attracting the attention of young men in the target age group required by the Army. One of the methods they employed to attract attention during the many fairs and fêtes they visited throughout the year was to construct a climbing wall. This was a vertical face along the surface of which were built randomly placed foot and toe holds. It was used to give the public a taste of basic climbing and abseiling. Naturally enough, regulations required of the nominated supervisors the requisite qualification – namely Top Roping and Abseiling Instructor.

Brittan had that qualification. Indeed he was a good all-round climber, strong, physically fit and had the benefit of having spent seven months in and around the jungles of Belize. Page, however, required that qualification in order to control the activities on the wall. It was whilst at the Army School of Adventurous Training at Ripon, Yorkshire, that he met Lieutenant Colonel Neill and Major Foster preparing themselves for their assault on Low's Gully. In between climbing and abseiling practice the two officers revealed their intention to Page. He expressed interest and eventually joined the team. Foster was then posted to Deepcut where Brittan, Page and their Mobile Display Team were based. Brittan was introduced to Foster. By all accounts, Foster was impressed by Brittan but, since all the slots had technically been filled, he was nominated as first reserve.

Mann, who worked on submarine repair in the Devonport Dockyard, was a part-time soldier in 383 Commando Troop (Petroleum Operations). When he walked into his Company office one day, the sergeant major told him of an offer to send a Territorial Army (TA) soldier to Malaysia to climb Mount Kinabalu. Now Mann nurtured a personal ambition to go to Hong Kong and he saw in this proposed exercise a means whereby his dream would come true. He declared an interest but, since nothing further developed he forgot about it, that is until he was asked again. Apparently a lieutenant colonel (Neill), who himself had served as a subaltern attached to the Royal Marines, wanted to take with him both a regular (Mayfield) and a Territorial Army representative. For Mann, the stumbling block initially appeared to be the five weeks he would need to take off work. Not overly optimistic, he thought he would feel the vibes at the dockyard. The response was amazingly supportive. His employers permitted him two weeks' TA leave, two weeks' annual leave, and one week 'on a course'. He then passed on to the next hurdle – his wife. 'I thought she would say no,' he admitted. His wife's response was surprisingly pragmatic: 'If they propose to pay you to go to Hong Kong, that's OK by me.'

In September of that Year, Neill wrote to Lieutenant Colonel D.J. Kerr, the then commanding officer of Supply Services Hong Kong, giving him the details of the expedition and offering three places. To help Kerr in his selection, Neill recommended that they should have 'a head for heights, an ability to swim and abseil'. No indication was given as to the arduous nature of the expedition. The invitation had only gone to Supply. In January 1994, Neill received the details of his three Hong Kong Chinese volunteers. Thus his team comprised ten men: one from York; one from Grantham, Lincolnshire; two from

Plymouth, Devon; two from Blackdown, Surrey; one from Waterbeach, Cambridge; and three from Hong Kong.

On 27 September 1993, Neill submitted his application to the authorities to lead the expedition to Kinabalu. The aim was:

> To complete the first descent of the north face of Mount Kinabalu, Sabah, by means of Low's Gully. Thereafter to follow the River Panataran to Kampong Melangkap Kappa (the nearest roadhead).

The exercise name was to be Exercise Gulley (sic) Heights Ebor. The practice is that adventurous training exercises are identified by two words and one other to designate the origin of the exercise. In this case, gully was misspelt. Ebor, an abbreviation of Eboracum, the Latin name for York, identified York as the location of Headquarters, Eastern District where Lieutenant Colonel Neill was a Grade One Staff Officer. By all accounts the relevant Army Training Department was mightily impressed by the precise manner in which Neill had submitted the application. But then, he had had practice. It was so good that there was some thought of using it as a model to guide future applicants. The form, however, only fulfils the administrative function of a check list. It does not and cannot make judgements as to whether the proposal is sensible or downright dangerous. To a large degree, that judgement has to be left to the leader. He is expected to strike the balance between reasonable and unreasonable risk. The commanding officer has a role to play in this process but, in a large Headquarters, a lieutenant colonel does not have a commanding officer *per se.* He has a superior officer, in this case a colonel, who is his reporting officer. However, a lieutenant colonel is also a senior officer in the British army and there is an expectation of him to get it right. The colonel would also have to rely upon the lieutenant colonel's judgement with regard to the suitability of other team members, the vast majority of whom in this case were based outside Eastern district and therefore beyond the colonel's bailiwick. The only other safety net is the local experience and knowledge of Defence Staff in the host country.

Neill had been told in September 1993 that political clearance might be problematical. Nevertheless, the Defence Attaché in Kuala Lumpur accepted the application to conduct Exercise Gulley Heights and passed copies to the Ministry of Defence and the Ministry of Tourism. Neill was warned by the Defence Attaché's office that he should not expect notification of the Malaysian authorities' approval until the last moment. His planned exercise dates were 18 February – 20 March 1994. Authorisation was eventually given on 16 February and Eastern District was signalled to that effect by the Defence Attaché. Eastern District in turn sent a priority signal to Supply Services, Hong Kong, for by then the team was already in the process of assembling in the Territory. It has been standard practice for the Malaysian authorities only to authorise adventure training exercises in their country immediately prior to the planned exercise start-date, irrespective of when the application reaches them. British Defence representation in South-East Asia has shrunk remarkably. For example, there are now no British defence staff at all in Manila, Philippines, despite that state's intention to rebuild its armed forces. The Defence Attaché in Kuala Lumpur is also responsible for the Philippines, and therefore it is unreasonable to expect him to have detailed knowledge of a parish spanning thousands of miles. Furthermore, he had not been long in post.

Two training sessions were planned for the seven members of the UK contingent. They assembled for the first time in Plymouth prior to going on to Dartmoor in Devon, 17–18 December 1993, to practise their rock climbing techniques, both at Dewerstone and on the Bickleigh Viaduct which offers a 140 ft free abseil. This session was run by Lance Corporal Mayfield, the group's rock climbing expert, who had also selected the venues.

Dartmoor was the first opportunity they had of assessing one another. There was an awareness that what they proposed to do was dangerous and therefore the team had to be interdependent. Brittan recalled his first impressions:

> What impressed me about Colonel Neill was the way he spoke. Everything was calculated, he paused between sentences, and generally gave a favourable impression that he had thought things through (Neill has a Law degree). Foster on the other hand was rather incongruous, reminiscent of an overweight grandpa, warm, softly spoken and friendly. He was poor on his skills. Mayfield, on the other hand, was technically brilliant and throughout our time there he gave a flawless performance.

Mayfield became the benchmark by which Brittan tested his own abilities. This meant that not only did group competition emerge but there would also be competition *within* what would become the advance group:

> Bob Mann looked fit and strong for his age. He was not technically brilliant yet he was extremely amusing. The fact that he was Territorial Army was obvious from the outset. He was so enthusiastic about the army, you know, so army barmy, to a degree that the regulars are not. Shearer was not there on that occasion but what was more important, neither was a Warrant Officer friend of Neill's and Foster's. He had dropped out, which meant that I was definitely in. My first impression of the team, therefore, was that we should have no real difficulties.

In the same way that the NCOs assessed one another, so did the officers examine each one of them. Arguably, the key figure among them was the highly qualified rock climbing expert, Lance Corporal Mayfield. By Neill's account he had the 'classic rock-climbing build'. Neill admitted to being slightly surprised that Mayfield was still a Lance Corporal. Yet Neill and Mayfield's commanding officer had been subalterns together in the Commando Logistic Regiment. It seems strange, therefore, that this somewhat obvious question was not raised earlier as part of the selection process. The men were obviously diffident in the presence of the two relatively senior and mature officers. They quickly got used to using their Christian names among themselves. Foster told them to call him 'Ron', but what to call Neill other than 'sir' or 'boss' was a hurdle yet to be crossed.

On 28 January, the party reassembled for two days at the Army School of Adventurous Training at Ripon, Yorkshire. Foster was absent, skiing in Germany. Because of delays and the poor weather conditions, no outdoor training was undertaken. It was prevented by driving rain and cold weather. Obviously they had assumed that in Borneo it wasn't going to get cold and they wouldn't be rained upon. In view of what was to happen, this was decidedly a missed opportunity. Instead, the time was given over to administration, the NCOs selecting and packing the British rations for the Chinese. The fact the team was so widely spread meant that there could be no group fitness and stamina training. No schedule or programme of fitness training was circulated, but individuals were advised of their own responsibility to prepare themselves for the exercise. Neill intended to practise the team and their individual skills over a three-day period in Hong Kong whilst *en route* to Kota Kinabalu. It all seemed a touch casual bearing in mind what the team proposed to do. The problem was that Neill and Foster had no clear idea what they were about to undertake. Both assumed that the reason the Gully had not been previously conquered was not due to the severe difficulty involved but rather that no one had got round to attempting it.

In *SOS*, Neill offers an unconvincing argument that, because the people he had seen over the period of two weekends were all mature NCOs, he was not disturbed by the fact that there had been no team training. Of the more important question of assimilation of the Chinese, Neill wrote that he was confident the 'Hong Kong lads would fit in'.

As part of his preparation at Ripon, Neill visited the Army's Adventurous Training School to discuss the nature and availability of equipment he should take with him. After a visit to the relevant Supply Depot at Thatcham, he was aware of what the shortfall was. Neill obtained authority to purchase large, hundred-litre capacity rucksacks in line with his philosophy of tackling Low's Gully – requiring a ten days' self-sufficiency, a 50 m rope and comprehensive climbing gear – which added up to more than twice the weight taken by New and Pinfield. The army also made available other, returnable items, such as lightweight tents and dive sacks*, but there was a small element on Neill's wish list which the team had to buy for itself – e.g. lightweight sleeping bags. The army's grant for the entire expedition was £2,660, while a further £1,000 came from regimental sources.

Foster was in charge of finance and had endeavoured to secure a sponsor for the exercise, but had failed. The fact that political clearance could not be guaranteed and was only given at the last moment meant that he could not book seats in advance on civil aircraft. Besides, the best deal he could strike was £6,000 – over twice the army grant – and that only got them as far as Hong Kong. The return air fare to Sabah would have been an additional £600 per person. He had bid through the system for seven air-trooping seats from London to Hong Kong and for ten air-trooping seats from Hong Kong to Brunei, Brunei being only 105 miles (170 kilometres) from Kota Kinabalu. These seats are allocated on a fill-up basis at no cost. Seats became available to fly the UK contingent to Hong Kong on 14 and 15 February 1994. Both groups moved in anticipation of political clearance which, as has been mentioned, was not forthcoming until the 16th. Foster left London on the first flight.

---

*A dive sack is a waterproof bag often associated with canoeing. In this case, the trekkers filled the bags with papers, wallets and other items they wished to keep dry and placed the closed dive sack inside their bergen rucksacks.

He arrived in Hong Kong on the evening of 15 February. In the space of the extra day he had available, he sought out additional equipment from Hong Kong's adventurous training pool, and met the three Hong Kong Chinese soldiers, Lance Corporal Cheung Yiu Keung (Cheung) who also used the name Kevin, (32), Private Lam Wai Ki (Lam or Victor), (27), and Private Chow Wai Keung (Chow), (24). Their command of English was not very good. According to them, Foster was told that none of them had done any training and they did not have the proper equipment. According to Cheung: 'He said not to worry, just bring some hiking kit as you will get some more specific equipment from England when you get to Brunei. He said we would be all right as we would train in Malaysia.' Good fortune smiled on the team, for exactly the right number of ten aircraft seats became available to take them all to Brunei on Wednesday 16 February.

A view has been expressed that the inclusion of the Hong Kong Chinese on this expedition was a ploy to gain benefits from Hong Kong. Examples of benefits quoted were: additional equipment, 'home advantage' in the allocation of seats to and from Brunei, and favourable consideration for rest and recuperation at the end of the exercise. Another opinion was that the inclusion of the Chinese in the team was due to 'the MOD's self-defeating, penny-pinching approach to adventure training'. However, there is a precedent of Hong Kong soldiers being included in Neill's exercises, albeit under different circumstances. Three hours after the second UK contingent arrived at Hong Kong's Kai Tak airport, they were all on the way to Brunei. In fact, the second party did not leave the airport but went into the transit lounge. The first time the entire group met was on the aircraft to Brunei.

A certain number of seats are pre-purchased by the Services on a Royal Brunei Boeing from Hong Kong to Brunei every Wednesday and Sunday. Therefore there was always a strong possibility that there would be no time for the team to get together in Hong Kong. They had not done their preparatory administration, established team harmony between the British and Chinese, or completed the planned three days' team training. That would now all have to be done in Sabah.

On the face of it, sympathy might otherwise be owing to the leader and his deputy had not the same happened on the Lancers' 1988 expedition, on which it will be recalled Foster was the driving force:

> The initial plan was to have a few days' acclimatisation in Hong Kong prior to deployment. This period of time had also been earmarked for progressive fitness training. This was not possible due to the availability of flights.

After their arrival in Brunei the expedition sought out accommodation, something they had not arranged from Hong Kong. They secured rooms in the Brunei Hotel at £25 a head. Despite having had no expense to date, and particularly having made savings by not having to pay for the flight to Brunei, the cost of a hotel room at £25 a night was thought to be excessive. The next day they moved out to an inexpensive and dilapidated youth hostel where they prepared their food and equipment for the passage of Low's Gully. At 7am on 18 February, they took a ferry to Labuan, where they changed to another, fast ferry to Kota Kinabalu. After two days of administration, where they stayed at the Traveller's Rest hostel, they hired a minibus to take them on to Kinabalu National Park, where they arrived on 20 February.

Neill was aware, both from his own experience and from what New had said, that there was no organised rescue service. He had considered this problem and determined that the group's security and well-being should come from within the group itself. It was a philosophy of 'safety in numbers', a philosophy which owed its whole rationale to the group staying together. Neill would provide Park Headquarters with an itinerary, indicating his intention to bring the ten-man team back to Park Headquarters on 4 March 1994. This date was critical, for Neill regarded it as a trigger date so that, in the event his team had not returned by 4 March, Park Headquarters would raise the alarm. In the event of an emergency, Neill gave as the point of contact 'Major Ramsden, Supply Services, BFPO 1, Hong Kong'. Neither Major Nigel Ramsden nor Hong Kong had been made aware of their role in a possible emergency situation, nor did Neill provide Park Headquarters with a contact telephone number.

The team's first priority was to bring the Hong Kong Chinese soldiers up to speed by teaching them to climb and descend single ropes. It is an enduring mystery why this had not been done earlier. An officer in Hong Kong said:

> From Osborne Barracks in Kowloon the Lion Rock can be seen, where most weekends Chinese rock climbers practise their skills, including hair-raising abseiling, training in which could (I assume) have been easily provided to the Hong Kong Chinese members of the team.

One of the second-floor, overhanging balconies of the New Fellowship Hostel, close to Park Headquarters, was used as a platform for a four-hour abseil training session, without rucksacks. It was here at the hostel that the British members of the group saw for the first time the limitations of their Chinese partners. One of them said: 'We could see that they hadn't done this before, other than Cheung who frankly was as good as Page and Mann. In all respects the other two were of recruit standard.' Neill spoke lightly of the importance of abseiling skill, saying it was a military skill that could be taught in five minutes. It is true that abseiling forms part of the Hong Kong soldiers' basic military training. However, in any military training conducted by objectives, once an objective is completed, a tick goes in the box and the subject is not revisited. 'To believe you can reasonably take soldiers down into Low's Gully after only five minutes' training, where you are all the while moving against the clock, is patent nonsense,' said the team member. 'Abseiling is a skill you develop. If you don't have that skill it can be a painfully slow process.' A further two-hour session was held up on the mountain.

One man who witnessed the training session being held at the New Fellowship Hostel on Sunday 20 February was David Powell, a British instructor with the Sabah Outward Bound School, who was also a director of a British travel company which specialises in activities associated with Kinabalu. Although he had not attempted Low's Gully, he obviously knew the mountain and the area very well. Powell was immediately concerned that anyone should contemplate going into Low's Gully with some of the team members demonstrating such poor standards of ability. Neill sought to reassure Powell by emphasising that both he and Foster had been on expeditions on Kinabalu before and *'had talked things through thoroughly with Robert New'.* In addition there was Mayfield, their experienced rock climber. If he and Neill felt satisfied with the Chinese after testing them up at the summit, they would accompany the team. Otherwise, they would be left behind. Powell told Neill of his concern and said that in his opinion their packs, weighing up to 95 lbs, were too heavy. He pointed out that there were porters available, and he offered a service to take the maximum permitted porter's load of 11 kilograms (25 lb) up to the Panar Laban huts. The price beyond 25 lb is negotiable with the porters. Although Neill had £360 available for such a contingency, he turned Powell's offer down.

Powell's was not the first warning Neill had received. The previous day, 19 February, at New's house, New expressed his concerns to Neill and Foster as to what they proposed to do. 'There were three concerns I did express. I mentioned them once and once only because I thought this was a proper expedition and not my place to intervene.' He too said the team's packs were too big and heavy. 'They would reduce general agility and put the trekkers in greater peril because they were then more likely to have an accident. You just do not have control of your body.' New's second concern was the size of the group. During his holiday in Sabah, Foster had invited New to join the expedition, an invitation that was repeated and again rejected. 'It depends on your philosophy,' explained New:

> There are two ends to the spectrum: the solo minimalist approach or the size of party involved in the conquest of Everest in 1953 with all the massive logistic considerations. I would not have enjoyed an expedition of the size proposed by Neill and Foster. When Pinfield and I decided to make our serious attempt on Low's Gully there was a third man, very well qualified indeed, who asked to join us. We said no because we believed a third man would increase the risk of injury within the trio by 50 per cent. I can see the logic in Neill's argument about safety in numbers: that more men can take more equipment, take with them a greater range of skills and have the numbers available to deal with an accident, but frankly I was not convinced.

But these considerations, although important, were not as important as the point with which New concluded. He told the expedition's leaders that, although technically they were within the dry season, the season had not quite begun. The rains were continuing. New said: 'I would not go down in this weather.' Once he had been in the Gully during a 5- to 10-minute period of light rain, which turned the trickle into a raging torrent:

> That scared us considerably. We came back determined to wait for a dry period which would guarantee us a week without rain. Such occasions do arise and we were prepared to wait a couple of years if necessary.

New had explained to his visitors that, with the weather remaining unpredictable, if rain were to fall on the bare summit it could cause serious, immediate complications in the Gully. In their book, Neill and Foster say their apprehensions had been lulled by the fact that no rain had fallen for several weeks 'and the wet season *appeared* to

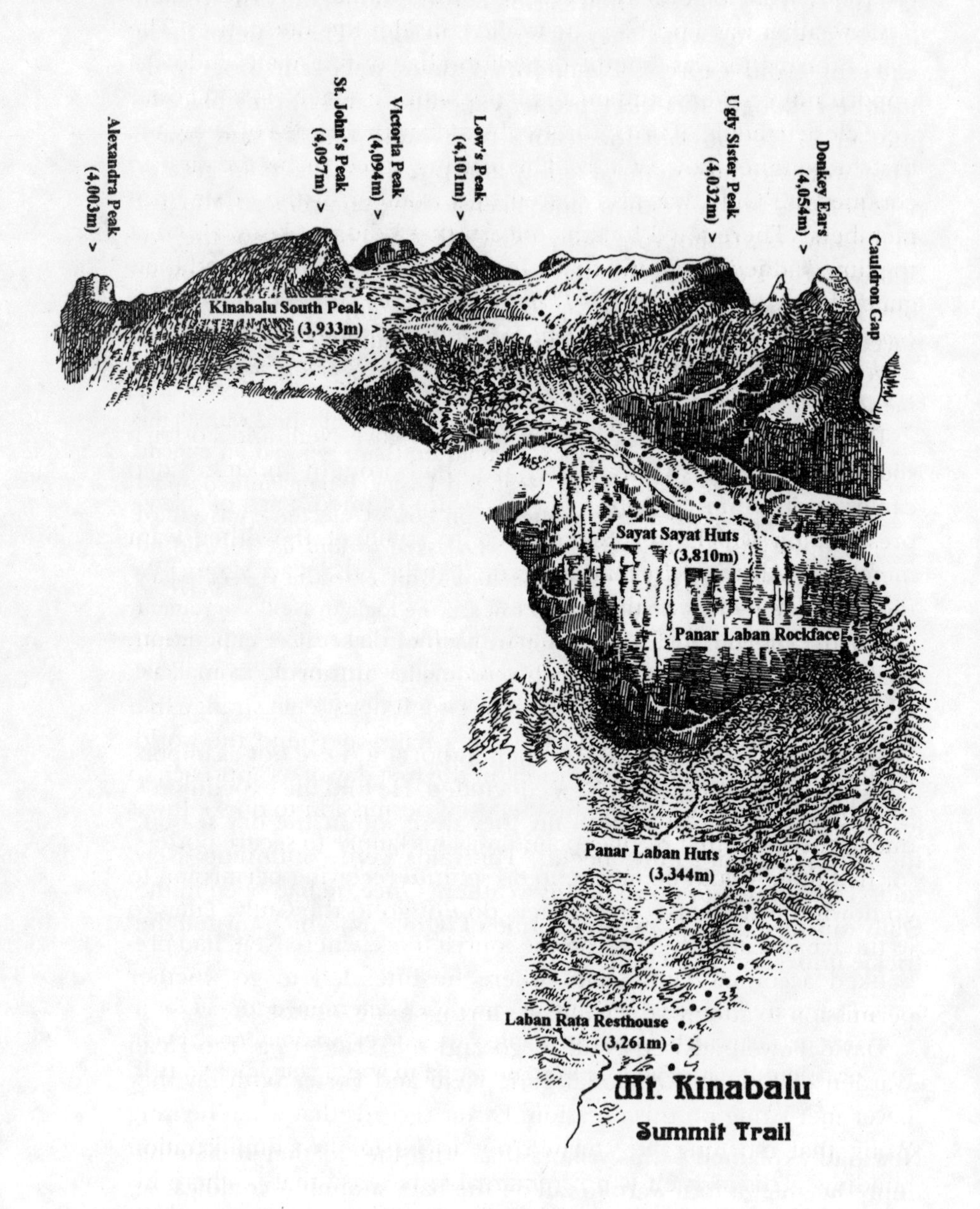
Alexandra Peak (4,003m) >
St. John's Peak (4,097m) >
Victoria Peak (4,094m) >
Low's Peak (4,101m) >
Ugly Sister Peak (4,032m) >
Donkey Ears (4,054m) >
Cauldron Gap
Kinabalu South Peak (3,933m) >
Sayat Sayat Huts (3,810m)
Panar Laban Rockface
Panar Laban Huts (3,344m)
Laban Rata Resthouse (3,261m)
Mt. Kinabalu
Summit Trail

be over' (my italics). New insists that he told them categorically that it was not. Neill as good as said to New, 'I hear what you say,' and that if the weather was a problem he would consider the alternatives. The fact of the matter was that the expedition had only a small window of opportunity on the mountain and it does appear that Neill and Foster were close to being, if not entirely, obsessed with the idea of being the first to conquer Low's Gully. This driving force to be the first to conquer the Gully was also shared by a number of the other team members. 'There was a fourth concern that I did not know about at the time,' added New, 'and that was the group composition and their general lack of experience.' *There is no mention in Neill's and Foster's book of the warning and advice that New gave to them. On the night of the 20th Neill rang his wife, telling her that he had seen New and was confident the abseils were within the team's capability.*

During the course of that evening, New gave Neill and Foster a slide show on Low's Gully. Foster, who had brought an 8mm video camera with him (a gift from his wife), filmed part of New's presentation which he then showed to some of the other team members. 'All the information seemed to be OK,' said Mann. 'We thought New had given the go-ahead.'

On the morning of 21 February, the first day of the expedition, Neill had still not received the requisite authority from Park Headquarters to proceed with the exercise. It does seem strange that after months of planning and travelling half way round the world, Neill should present his expedition on the first day of its approach to the objective without having first secured permission to do so. It was due to this lapse that Neill explains away his failure to secure porters, for he felt he would be unwise to do so until receiving permission to go down the Gully. But the porters do not go to the Gully. They go to the Panar Laban huts up on the tourist track, where Neill had pre-booked accommodation, and where he intended to go whether permission to attempt the Gully was forthcoming, or not.

David Powell advised Neill to go and see Eric Wong, the Head Warden of Kinabalu National Park. Neill and Foster both say they never met Wong on this occasion. Foster records that when he rang Wong that morning, he 'turned out to be in the administration building'. This in itself is not remarkable because that is where his office is! He was said to have invited the two officers to come and see him, and both were driven the short distance by Powell. Allegedly, when they arrived at Wong's office someone was with him so they were attended to by a deputy. The book recalls how Neill 'bitterly' regretted not insisting on meeting Wong, but argues that it would have been difficult to have done so because he was 'a guest in the Park Headquarters'. The suggestion is that had Neill done so, the personal contact might have resolved some of the problems when the expedition became overdue. The reason why Neill did not wait until Wong's supposed visitor left is not explained. Nor why Wong, who was obviously expecting them, did not see them. Wong insists that it was he who met and dealt with the two officers, not a deputy. 'Neill showed me a letter he had written some months previously to our Kota Kinabalu office,' said Wong,

> in which he requested permission to go into Low's Gully and come out at the Panataran River. He claimed he had not had an answer, but here he was with his team, ready to go. It was difficult for me to say no, but these instances are not unusual.

Wong took photocopies of Neill's and Foster's passports and, as one who had been in the Park for 21 years, he was in the best position to discuss and advise on their aspirations. He pointed out the availability of porters who would go as far as Panar Laban:

> When I heard what they wanted to do and the time they had allowed, I told them what they proposed was over-ambitious. I did not think it possible for them to achieve what they wanted in one week. I have climbed up towards Low's Gully with heavy packs on what was intended to be a 10-day mission from the Panataran River to 4,000 feet. We could not go any further because we had neither sufficient equipment nor time to proceed. Our progress was greatly impeded by a flood which meant it took four days to get to 4,000 feet. But then going along the river we were not as restricted as we would have been in the Gully, where options do not exist.

Wong insisted that they should think about having to take longer and, by implication, take more rations. The Britons had not put themselves in the best of positions to respond to this advice, but Neill agreed that if there were insurmountable difficulties up above, he might look at something less ambitious. Neill then signed a form of indemnity, absolving the Park authorities from any claim which might arise as a result of the expedition. He picked up his permit and obtained insurance cover before leaving Park Headquarters at 5,200 feet (1,561 metres) just after 9am.

Delayed as they were by the last-minute administration, the team was pleased to accept an offer of a lift from Powell, who shuttled them and their equipment up the steep tarmac road as far as the power station at 6,200 feet (1,890 metres). This is a small diesel-fired station which provides electricity for the installations on the mountain. Neill considered the offer of Powell's lift to have been a better option than hiring porters, but then, he could have arranged to make rendezvous with the porters at the power station. It was not an either/or situation.

Powell was at the Gunting Lagadan Hut in the Panar Laban group on the evening of 21 February and saw the expedition members arrive. He happened to be looking out of the window when he saw the first few. He remembers thinking 'they did that in good time,' but what he did not know was that the other six were still strung out down the mountain path. From the state of the stragglers, he just could not envisage how they were going to complete their mission. He confided in Neill his concerns as to the expedition's safety, and strongly advised, even at this late stage, against taking the team into Low's Gully. The next day he offered to raise the alarm if he had not heard from them by a given day. 'Give me a day and a date,' he said. That offer was declined. Even at the summit on 23 February, Powell recommended to Neill and Foster that they should reconsider what they proposed to do. He tried to impress upon them the difficulty of what they were attempting to achieve:

> I do not believe Neill knew what he was doing. I had already advised him at the bottom to tip out the four litres of water each man was carrying, for since his last expedition ten years before, water points have been set up along the way. (It seems that the group did know of the water points but carried the water until they could ascertain for themselves exactly what the water availability and quality were like.) When Foster came out for his recce he didn't go past the Park HQ. They didn't know, for example, of the addition of the comfortable Laban Rata guest house to the list of available accommodation.

Powell's constant insistence on caution and suggestion that there were less dangerous challenges up at the summit were clearly beginning to get under Neill's skin. At their last meeting on 22 February, Neill asked Powell: 'Have you ever been into Low's Gully?' 'No,' admitted Powell. 'Well, how do you know it is as horrendous as you claim?' 'I have heard what Robert New has had to say,' said Powell. 'I spent an evening with New two days ago,' countered Neill, failing to mention that New had said much the same as Powell was now saying. Then Neill asked Powell: 'Have you ever been on the Panataran River?' On being told 'no', Neill said *he* had, and Foster had been there three times. But the Panataran River was not Low's Gully, and the two officers' performance there could hardly have been described as having been a success.

In their book, Neill and Foster remark how Powell was on shaky ground in trying to 'influence the course of a military expedition'. Put simply, they did not rate the Outward Bound instructor highly. But Powell would be proved to be right. Moreover, Sergeant Mann (the third most senior member of the expedition), Lance Corporal Mayfield (the expert climber), and the three Chinese soldiers, all endeavoured to change the course of an evolving military expedition in which they were rapidly losing confidence.

3

An Inauspicious Start

The power station at 6,200 ft (1,890 metres) is the beginning of the tourist trail up to the summit. Here, the expedition left Powell's minibus. He helped them take their bergens out of the vehicle. 'I could barely lift them,' he said. 'I wouldn't dream of carrying them.' He watched the team jostle with their heavy blue rucksacks while Neill instructed them to make their own way to the Panar Laban Huts at 11,000 ft (3,344 m) – a climb of 3,700 ft over a distance of two and three-quarter miles (4½ km). Powell turned to the tourist group he was accompanying and said of Neill's party, 'someone is going to die'. Thus, at the very beginning, the team was encouraged to break up into its ability groups. The recognition that there were considerable ability differences and differences in levels of fitness was reflected in the manner in which the team was paired off to carry their share of group equipment: Neill and Foster, Mann and Mayfield, Brittan and Page, Cheung and Shearer, Chow and Lam. The team was riven by a whole cocktail of divisive factors. The Chinese soldiers were never fully integrated into the team. Foster and Mann were territorial soldiers while the rest were regular servicemen. Among the regulars were a soldier/commando and a para, whose units regard themselves as elitist and whose members are not unknown to look down their noses at members of regiments they regard as inferior. Then there was the age difference. Over half the group individually were under half the age of Foster, and Foster's and Neill's combined age was 100 years. Instead of going up the mountain together as a team, individuals were told to go at their own pace so as to enjoy the ascent. It was already 9.30am. The expedition should have been well on its way by this time instead of fussing about administration which should have been pre-arranged.

Given these disparities it would have been prudent to have done more to bond the team, to raise team spirit. The British component did meet on two occasions for training and administration – sufficient time to form an impression of each other's merits and capabilities, which is so essential in developing mutual confidence. The Chinese were an unknown quantity. A practice exercise for the whole team and reserves would not have been unusual for an expedition proposing to undertake such a difficult mission. This would certainly have given the Chinese soldiers an earlier opportunity to discover the arduous nature of the exercise and that, through no fault of their own, they were unprepared and out of their depth. Neill did recognise the fact that he had three defined groups within his team: the keen, young and fit men, the 'whippets'; the 'oldies'; and the novice Chinese soldiers. His intended *modus operandi* was to engage the whippets as his forward reconnaissance, acting as his eyes and ears, returning on a regular basis with information as to what lay ahead. There is no doubt that he intended to maintain the integrity of the group. The forays and returns of the whippets from their reconnoitring being described as the 'elastic band' principle. 'I and Major Foster were the oldies,' explained Neill,

> ... the brains. The Chinese were the novices and the NCOs were my whippets. They were the youngest, fittest blokes who were my eyes and ears. They were the ones who would run about at my command, fixing ropes, finding escape routes.

This was a policy not without its flaws: firstly, the group had no radio of any description and therefore they could not inter-communicate; secondly, the leadership would be leading from the rear; and thirdly, there was only one rock climber of any significance in the group, so where should he be? Forward with the reconnaissance, or in the rear to assist the novices and the relatively elderly? If there is one golden rule for an expedition setting out into unknown territory it is 'don't split up'. Yet Neill had assembled a group riven with numerous fault lines, just waiting to crack under the strain. Good communications within the group might have prevented the fault lines from parting, but this was not to be the case. The damage took place in the early stages of the exercise. As the team climbed the mountain, so it divided.

Neill had asked Mann to video the start as they passed under the ornamental wooden arch to the side of the power station. Mann kept his video equipment in a yellow, airtight case, 'the yellow peril'. In Plymouth, he had phoned a number of companies for quotations to supply a box for his £1,000 camera and films. He gave them dimensions which would allow the gear to fit inside the box, but what he had neglected to do was to check that the box would fit inside his bergen. It did not. To save face he took it, but it had to be strapped to the top of his bergen. After filming 'the off', Mann put away the camera and ran the 500 metres to catch up with the back markers. At first Mayfield stayed with him, but Mann insisted that he should press on. Needing no second invitation, Mayfield moved swiftly up the slope towards the front. Neill's assumption that the team would more or less stay together, particularly the pairs, was shown to be misconstrued from the start. Mann had not gone many yards before he became aware that this was a hard slog. He had on his back his own kit, his quota of shared kit and 26 lb of camera equipment. Quite a burden for someone of nine and a half stone.

Now Mann knew that he was fit for his age, yet he had some underlying doubts as to whether his age would count against him. In Brunei they had had to walk the quarter-mile from their accommodation to the ferry:

> Major Foster had already recced the route for fences and rails upon which to rest our packs. We also had suitcases. When we got to the boat it took two porters to lift each bergen aboard. Major Foster was sweating like hell, he's a big man. Up until then I assumed that if anyone would be holding anyone back, it would be me. It's not that I can't keep up, but at my age it takes longer to recover. When I saw the state of the major, I was not worried about it from that point on. I looked at the Chinese lads. They seemed fit youngsters. Cheung is a physical training instructor, so I thought they'd be OK. I had obviously worried myself unduly. I was so naïve!

In the first group moving up the mountain were Mayfield, Brittan, Shearer, Page, Cheung and Lam. Mayfield and Brittan tested their own abilities one against the other. Their competition drew them away even from the advance group, for whom they had to stop and wait 40 minutes. Bringing up the rear, pacing themselves, were Neill, Foster and Mann, with Chow isolated between the two groups. The advance party reached the Panar Laban Huts at 4.30pm. Although it was light for a further two hours, Neill was becoming concerned that his tail-end group would not reach the hut in daylight. His solution was to leave some of his party's equipment by the track with a view to returning to collect it in the morning.

Mann was not at all happy about leaving his kit behind. In his view, they had head torches and could have continued, but he admitted inwardly that he had thought 'thank Christ for that'. They put half their kit into dive sacks which they hid in the hedge. Neill said, 'I'll be interested to know who out of the younger ones will come back to see where we are.' Mann replied that, out of all of them, 'Richard (Mayfield) will come back.' The Colonel looked at Mann strangely, quizzically, but said nothing. Mann thought about this silent exchange, arguing with himself, 'well, why shouldn't he? In 3 Commando Brigade you look after one another.'

After taking tea which Neill had brewed, they continued the climb, making better progress than if they had been encumbered with full bergens. As Mann led the group around a corner, he came across a man lying on the track on his back, 'turtle up'. It was Chow. As soon as he saw him, he recognised the effects of dehydration and exhaustion. 'He'd had it,' said Mann, who took the bergen off the soldier's back and shouted to the colonel coming up behind. Mann used some water to bring Chow around and also fed him some chocolate. When Neill arrived on the scene, he hit the roof. 'What the hell's he doing here by himself?', he demanded. Neill had assumed that the three Chinese would keep together. They took out half his kit and put that in a hedge. Mann said to Neill that Chow was totally incapable of carrying even half a load. But he needed his kit for the night. Mann suggested that Neill, Foster and Chow should go on ahead, leaving Chow's half load with him. He asked Neill to send one of the others back down the track to help him with Chow's bergen.

By the time Chow had been sorted out it was already dusk. As Mann sat by the track, alone except for two half bergens, the darkness intensified. Within 15 minutes of being there alone, he was struck by the spookiness of the place. He thought he heard sounds and eery rustlings off the track and all around him. He took out his head torch and turned it on. Then he took out a cigarette and lit it. He thought to himself that he ought to pack up smoking – his breathing had become laboured. After a very short period, he decided that he wasn't going to sit there doing nothing, so he took one bergen at a time 300 ft up the track, a process known as pepper-potting. In the space of one hour, Mann had got himself into a state similar to

Chow's, severely affected by altitude. He had physically exhausted himself so that by the time help eventually arrived, he could not breathe. He felt as though his heart was being ripped from his chest. Mann tried to carry his half load but could not manage it. The three who had come down to help carried his and Chow's, but Mann still found himself unable to keep up as he fought to get air into his lungs.

Neill and Chow reached the hut at 7pm. Foster came in as the back marker. He was accompanied by the ubiquitous Powell who had seen his distressed state and carried his equipment the 300 ft between their respective accommodation. Neill's mood was one of anger. According to Foster, he gave the forward party 'a good bollocking'. The Colonel made it absolutely clear that he would not tolerate 'every man for himself'. They were accused of having abandoned Chow. Neill ordered Mayfield, Shearer and Brittan to go back down the track to help Mann with Chow's gear. Then Neill went to seek out Chow's two Chinese colleagues, Cheung and Lam. He gave them the unrestrained benefit of his thoughts, finally ordering them to prepare sweet tea for Chow and to ensure he went into his sleeping bag and rested. This was a defining moment for the expedition, affecting as it did the balance and the mood within the group. The expedition was mortally wounded, never to recover. After all, the NCOs were also tired after their climb. The Chow incident had really been an oversight, it being assumed by those in front that he had fallen back to accompany the oldies. When Mann entered the hut:

> you could have cut the atmosphere with a knife. I could feel the friction between certain members of the group. I can understand the colonel getting ratty because a member had been left behind and I can also understand the others getting ratty, but if you get a bollocking you just have to take it on board.

Mayfield, the soldier/marine, was particulary nonplussed at being the focal point of his leader's displeasure when the leader's clear instructions had been for them to make their own way to Panar Laban, with the assurance that he would be bringing up the rear. Mayfield was already nursing his own personal disquiet regarding the poor physical state of some of the team members, and doubts as to whether they should be allowed to proceed into Easy Valley.

During the evening, a second exchange occurred between Neill and Mayfield. Where the spark between them had grown is not clear.

Mayfield, tall, youthful and quiet by nature, was the climbing expert, Neill was not. Mayfield had gone to Neill's and Foster's room. Foster was there, still suffering the effects of his exertion up the mountain. Mayfield asked Foster if he might talk to him. Foster agreed, but at that point Neill entered the room. 'Can you give me five minutes alone, sir?', asked Mayfield. 'I would like five minutes alone with Ron.' Neill refused. He told Mayfield that if he had anything to say to Foster, he should say it in front of both of them, arguing that he did not have any secrets from his deputy.

Mayfield appeared agitated. He had been severely shaken by the expedition's performance on the climb up the tourist track to the accommodation and thought that he, as the best-qualified climber in the group, should offer his advice. He wanted a diplomatic moment alone with Foster who, he believed, was not up to taking part in the expedition. Neill's uncompromising position meant that he could not discuss his concerns with Foster without being acutely embarrassed.

According to one who was there, Mayfield 'threw his teddy into the corner' and stormed out of Neill's room. The others heard Neill shout 'Richard, Richard, come back', while Mayfield, his face like thunder, ignored Neill and left the building for the restaurant below. Foster who, quite correctly, believed he was to be quizzed about his fitness, thanked Neill for his timely intervention. Foster had no doubts in his own mind about his physical fitness. Brittan's view was that Mayfield's professional opinion should have been listened to:

> He is, after all, a Joint Service Rock Climbing Instructor and in terms of what we were about to do, the best person to make and give a professional judgement. His word should have been heeded, but it wasn't and he simply wound his neck in.

Mayfield's situation was difficult, to say the least. He was a young man who had a professional opinion about what he and the group were expected to do. Neill was not only almost twice his age but also a senior officer. Mayfield would not have had the experience of dealing so closely with senior officers, certainly not those who had a different leadership style from that to which he was accustomed.

The use of Christian or forenames on expeditions or during team games in the Services is a moot point. Some team leaders allow it as a matter of course while others see it as being inappropriate. It is certainly something the military hierarchy frown upon and actively discourage. However in the case of this exercise, even one of the caves was called after Cheung's English name – Kevin. On this expedition there was an undoubted dichotomy between Neill's insistence that the team members were on a military exercise and his attempt at achieving informality through such means as the use of Christian names, justified on the basis that on the expedition they were as good as civilians. He told his men that his name was Robert and Foster's was Ron. Those who deplore such familiarity across the rank structure would argue that this is a manifestation of the thin end of the wedge. When things really get tough, leadership and discipline will be found to have been undermined because subordinates can become less respectful and considerate of their superiors. One survival expert, Hugh McManners, summed up the consensus view:

> Army rank and responsibility are earned, and paid for, and should not be discarded or ignored. Until subordinates come to respect those in authority in person, they must respect their rank. They are not entitled to suspend that respect – and they know it.

There is no divine right to respect, it has to be earned.

> When people are getting to know each other under the pressure of doing something dangerous, you need as much social structure as possible. Without it, even in military expeditions, an aggressive Darwinian anarchy can develop – literally, the survival of the fittest.

Mann and Mayfield shared the same room. While Mayfield cooked Mann a meal, they talked. Mann heard of the bollocking and argument. The day's events had been a short, sharp shock to Mann who earnestly contemplated exactly what they were on about. As soon as he had recovered, he asked Neill if they could have 'an O group' (meeting) at 9pm. He had at the back of his mind what he thought needed to be said, but wanted more time to think it through. He opened his notebook and wrote down six names, and some ideas he had gleaned from Neill's 1982 expedition. He remembered having read about the group dividing, and put down a form of words in such a manner as not to upset any party. His suggestion was that the four most able men should go down into the Gully, to be met at the bottom by the other six 'mules' providing essential support. When finished, he spoke to Mayfield. Firstly, he suggested to Mayfield that, if he had any qualms about Neill's plans it would be best for all concerned if he put his misgivings through Mann, the TA sergeant. The second matter he wanted to air was the six men he had identified as not being up to it. They were the three Chinese (he had a question mark against Cheung), Neill, Foster and Mann himself.

After listening to what Mann proposed to tell Neill, Mayfield said, 'Bob, you've hit the nail right on the head.' For Mann, it had been extremely hard to include his own name on the list. He had set out on the expedition with the intention of being able to tell his grandchildren of having been the first to conquer Low's Gully. He hadn't even reached the Gully. To exclude himself voluntarily from something he had gone half-way round the world to achieve was difficult, yet he was able to rationalise his decision on the grounds that he would still be a member of the first team to conquer Low's Gully. After all, only two members of the 1953 Everest expedition reached the summit. Mayfield, appreciative of the proposed sacrifice, said simply 'cheers for doing that'.

The meeting convened, as directed. On Neill's left sat Foster, on his right, Mann, with the others in between. Mann sensed that the colonel knew he was about to come out with something. When he attempted to speak first, Neill interjected: 'This is my O Group and we'll do it my way.' Those around the table recognised that the colonel was out to restore his authority as the team leader. Neill apologised for not hiring porters and admitted that with hindsight he should have done so. But then he went on to examine his reasons for not having done so. Apparently the lateness of the day meant that there were no porters available. Powell's offer was not mentioned. (But since, a few hours before, Neill had seen Mayfield in earnest discussion with Powell, it was an association not likely to raise either man in Neill's estimation.) Neill then rehearsed his displeasure at what had happened to Chow. In a stick and carrot monologue he deprecated any manifestation of 'I'm all right Jackmanship', saying that they should remember that although this was an expedition it was still, foremost, a military exercise, at the conclusion of which he would be sending reports to their commanding officers. But he softened the implied threat by assuring them that nothing had occurred thus far to raise any adverse comment.

Neill then emphasised that it was *his* expedition and that *he* was the leader. Those sitting around the table all had their own specific roles to play. Mayfield, for example, was the climbing expert and in that environment he was 'king', but as far as the expedition's safety was concerned, that was the leader's responsibility and his alone. Neill admitted to having some reservations with Chow's fitness but he believed, with the climb up the mountain, the worst of the physical activity was behind them. Neill, who had wanted them to enjoy the ascent, expressed a wish that they should now enjoy – by implication – the easier task of descending into Low's Gully.

After his monologue, Neill, skipping Foster, went clockwise round the table asking those present to speak their minds. There are variations of emphasis upon exactly what was said that evening. What follows is as close a representation as is possible. Chow had been severely embarrassed by his collapse. He apologised and restated what he had said to Mayfield to the effect that he was not fit enough to continue. Not unreasonably under the circumstances, Neill persuaded Chow to continue. For the most part, the Chinese did not understand what was going on because the participants spoke too quickly. When it came to Mayfield's turn he said that he was concerned about certain members of the group, adding that he was responsible for the safety of the team and that that was something he felt he could not guarantee. The tone of Neill's response to Mayfield was described as 'savage'. According to one present, he said:

> I am the expedition leader, Major Foster is my deputy, you are my rock climbing expert. On any matters of climbing I will listen to you and evaluate everything you say, but the safety of this group is not your responsibility. That is mine, and mine alone.

Mayfield was apparently also excluded from advising on anything pertaining to abseiling, because Neill and Foster were both qualified. Neill had already formed the impression that Mayfield believed he should be deputy leader rather than Foster. Brittan, who would have supported the Mann plan, cautioned: 'If we are to continue, it is important that we stay within our capabilities.'

Then it came to Mann's turn. The atmosphere in the room was distinctly frigid. Mann was not certain that what he had to say would calm things down. Moreover, he was concerned that what he had to say would sound stupid. Slowly and deliberately he took out his notebook, to which he referred as he spoke in his soft, West Country accent:

> What I am about to say may either upset or annoy certain members of the group, but I feel it has to be said. I feel that certain members of the expedition are not up to the required standard to achieve our aim. Our aim is to be the first ever to traverse Low's Gully and make history.

He then outlined his plan to those seated round the table. He told them how the whole group ought to go to the summit, with four, possibly five, going over the top into the Gully while the other five or six would map and reconnoitre the mountain for three days before going back down the mountain and up the Panataran River to the bottom of the Gully, to meet the others coming down. The five or six on the circuitous route would carry additional rations so as to be able to replenish the group coming out of the Gully. The real problems of making rendezvous down there were still not fully appreciated. Nevertheless, Mann thought this better than what seemed to be the Colonel's 'do or die' proposal, arguing that it would still achieve the team's aim, thereby reflecting great credit upon the Royal Logistic Corps. Then came the difficult part: proposing the names of those who would be in the diversionary, logistic support group. Mann had put his name at the top of the list. He then read out the Colonel's, the Major's and the Chinese names.

Neill replied evenly, saying he had listened carefully to what had been said. He complimented Mann on his delivery. If there were any problems, he said, the option existed to do other things. However, he reminded the group that he had been into Easy Valley and had also come up the Gully from the river. 'So has Major Foster and I feel, as does Major Foster, that we are all capable, and that includes you Chinese, of beating the Gully.' In *SOS*, Neill rejects the Panataran River approach on the grounds that, during previous expeditions, the team members had been unable to negotiate the rain-swollen river. Yet, by their earlier admission, they were content to enter the Gully on the basis of their assessment that the wet season had ended. Neill had argued that the difficult part was now behind them. Their bergens would lighten as they consumed their rations, and the altitude's debilitating influences would progressively recede. No one doubted that the Colonel was genuinely convinced that they could defeat Low's Gully.

In view of the difficulties experienced that day, and Powell's intercessions having some effect, Neill declared the next day, 22 February, to be a rest day, during which those who had left equipment lower down the track were expected to take the opportunity to recover it. The whippets then asked if they might have permission to look around the summit and go into Easy Valley, to which the reply was in the affirmative. It is of interest that Mayfield had sought permission from Foster because he was not on speaking terms with Neill. The meeting broke up and Neill took the aggrieved Mayfield aside. Although a form of apology from the marine was forthcoming, it was evident that if in future these two rubbed up against one another, a flash might be the inevitable consequence.

It may be that Neill was content that he had stamped his authority on the group, but one of the team remarked how, on leaving the table, he had thought in his heart of hearts, 'bloody hell'. Mann said that:

> with hindsight, and as we would see, Mayfield was right in everything he said. He was not trying to undermine authority, it's the way he goes about things, he's just not a diplomat. I had doubts when we left the table that night.

Foster felt the same unease: 'It is hard not to think that the seeds which were eventually to divide the expedition were sown here.'

The evening provided the opportunity for quiet contemplation. This was particularly true of the Chinese soldiers. They did not feel part of the team. But then, even the British members had not had time to feel they were part of the team. The Chinese, on top of that, had language and culture differences to consider. If they couldn't get up the hill, argued Corporal Brittan, what would they be like over the other side? There can be no doubt that a number of the British soldiers had come to the very early conclusion that the Chinese novices represented such a severe handicap as to threaten the expedition's mission of being the first to descend Low's Gully.

The Chinese soldiers came to that same conclusion during the night. Next morning, all three faced up to Neill and requested that they go no further. They argued that their relative unfitness and unpreparedness for what they were expected to undertake would prejudice the entire expedition. Neill was persuasive – almost persuasive – for Cheung returned in the company of Mann to re-state his case, but to no avail. Apparently Neill had told them that the difficulties were all part of their character-building; difficulties to conquer. According to Cheung, Neill said to them: 'You are soldiers and you can and must go down the Gully. If you don't, you will be sent back to Hong Kong and your Colonel will be informed and there may be some punishment.' He told them how they had been hand-picked by Lieutenant Colonel Kerr for the express purpose of going down the Gully, but he didn't say that he had given their commanding officer only the barest outline as to what they would be up against. Besides, said Neill reassuringly, other Chinese soldiers before them had done much the same thing on earlier expeditions. Earlier expeditions had been nothing like the descent into what came so close to becoming a valley of death. Anyway, he said, the team would go at their pace. Neill had still not comprehended that New and Pinfield had been whippets *par excellence.* He had made a far too optimistic assessment both of the difficulties and his people's capabilities. On the morning of 22 February, Neill, Foster, Mann and Chow went back to collect kit and also to look at the large, overhanging rock where Hugh Low had spent the night on the mountain in 1851.

Mayfield put on his trainers and took with him his small bergen and sufficient kit with which to stay out all night if need be, although it was his intention to be gone only five or six hours. Off he went to reconnoitre Easy Valley. He ran up to the Sayat-Sayat Hut, from where he looked over the abyss into the Cauldron. He got vertigo and decided not to look again. Then he descended 2,000 ft into Easy Valley, to a point which he believed Neill had reached. Looking down, he thought he could see the bottom of the valley and believed the task looked quite easy, 'patches of jungle and the odd steep bit, but nothing too drastic'. He ran back up the hill, considerably more reassured than he had been the previous day. When he reported in, he declared himself to be 'quite happy'. 'Well I wasn't quite happy but I could understand that it was the colonel's show and if he wanted to take everybody, then, well it was his responsibility.' His residual reservations concerned the technical ability of Neill, Foster, Mann and the three Chinese.

The tension developing between the British and the Chinese soldiers came to a head in the late afternoon of the 22nd. During the course of the final inspection of kit and equipment, the British soldiers formed the opinion that the Chinese soldiers did not have their essential scale of rations. To some, a deficiency seemed to have occurred between this, the final inspection, and an inspection held previously at Kota Kinabalu. One suggestion, false as it transpired, was that the Chinese soldiers had, *en route,* disposed of some of their food in order to lighten their packs. This thought was then drawn to the attention of the officers. What on the face of it should have been nothing more than a storm in a teacup did become, due to unimaginable stupidity, a future matter of unnecessary political significance. So what really happened over the vexed question of disappearing rations?

The rations epitomised the 'make do' nature of so many adventurous training exercises. The food had come over as freight on the same plane as the team. It was a mix of 10-man British ration packs and some Gurkha rations. There was more food than they could possibly need. Individuals had also brought with them their own favourites as supplements. The sorting of the food in Brunei was one of the first tasks to be undertaken. The members of the team were told to extract ten days' rations from the pile. To each Chinese soldier there was a British soldier nominated to assist. Now the Chinese do not eat the type or quantity of food eaten by the British. They did not recognise, or want, canned steak and kidney pudding. They eat noodles and had each purchased ten packets in Kota Kinabalu. Cheung could keep going for days on the same amount of food that would sustain Brittan for hours. The point is that the Chinese would not know what constituted ten days' food in the format lying in front of them. Mann, not for a moment thinking 'I'm British, he's Chinese', told Lam, 'out of these boxes, Victor, get 10 days' rations', and left it at that.

In the Traveller's Rest hostel at Kota Kinabalu, the Colonel had told the three 'minders' to strip the Chinese soldiers' equipment and double check that they had 10 days' rations. To his horror, Mann had found that Lam had with him five days' food at the most. 'Victor, what are you doing? It's not enough.' He then showed Lam the quantity which would comprise one day's rations. 'Get another five, you need ten in all.' Lam turned to the sergeant in exasperation: 'But Bob, I can't eat this and I don't like that'. To which Mann replied, 'Well substitute it for noodles'. Mann admits that had he been dealing with a recruit, he would have gone back to double check. 'I assumed he was a trained soldier with a fair amount of experience. What he did then was to put together as best he could what he thought 10 days' rations would be.'

On the evening of 22 February, the rest day, Neill ordered the Chinese rations to be rechecked. 'When the kit was laid out', recalled Brittan, 'one of our number cast an interested eye over it and blurted out "look at their rations – that's not enough to get them through 10 days".' Mann, not present at the time, was drawn to the scene by the ongoing commotion. 'The Colonel was ranting and raving and Lam and Chow were also ranting and raving, in Chinese.' Mann looked down at Lam's modest collection of food. 'Victor, where are your rations?', he demanded.

Incredulous and excited, Lam pointed to the same pile, 'there Bob, there Bob!'.

The Chinese connection had not been sufficiently thought through at the beginning for this problem represented a fundamental breakdown in communications. The Chinese soldiers simply could not comprehend the reason for the great excitability going on around them. Lam's pile was smaller than it had been in Kota Kinabalu before it had been supposedly topped up. He had no more than four days' rations. One of those responsible for checking the rations then said, 'they've obviously chucked them away to lighten their packs'. As Mann explained, the accusation was logical but wrong. None of the others had seen the Chinese eating the rations earlier that evening because at that time they were in the restaurant. The British understood that they only drew on their rations when they went over the lip, into the Gully. No one had explained this to the novices, who assumed that Day 1 of the exercise was the day they left Kota Kinabalu. Neill ordered them to go down to the café shop to buy more rations. He gave each of them 50 Malaysian dollars from exercise funds. They returned, having bought the café out of noodles, sardines and chocolate, but still had insufficient food. Mayfield and Mann then came forward to hand over their 24 hour emergency rations and certain less popular everyday rations such as hard tack biscuits – something they would have given much for two weeks later.

Neill took Cheung into a corner where he expressed his disappointment at Cheung's and the others' behaviour. Cheung did not refute the claims that he and his compatriots had dumped rations. He did not comprehend what he was being accused of and was therefore totally perplexed by his admonition. Many weeks later, at the Board of Inquiry, his accusers were noted to be visibly crestfallen and repentant of their stupidity. This silly business symbolised a major, underlying problem of communication. No one had worked out that the Chinese did not eat British food, that they may not have had money to buy food, and that they lived an entirely different way of life. Both Neill and Foster had had previous service with Hong Kong soldiers.

Neill declared that the next morning, the 23rd, the whole group would go up to Low's Peak to watch the sunrise. The plan was for all to take a half load up to the Sayat-Sayat Huts, where the packs were to be hidden, before proceeding on to the summit. Here they would

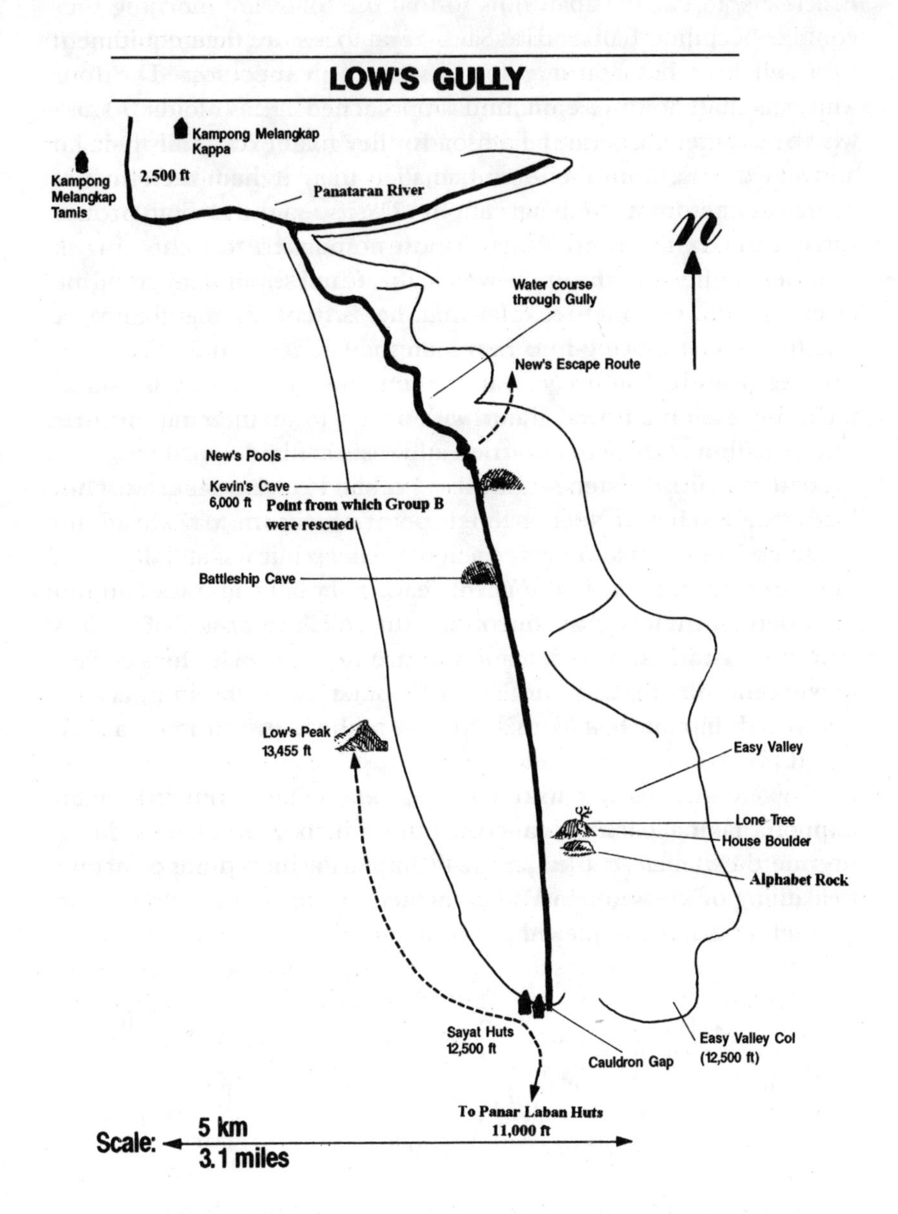
LOW'S GULLY
Kampong Melangkap Kappa
Kampong Melangkap Tamis
2,500 ft
Panataran River
n
Water course through Gully
New's Escape Route
New's Pools
Kevin's Cave 6,000 ft
Point from which Group B were rescued
Battleship Cave
Low's Peak 13,455 ft
Easy Valley
Lone Tree
House Boulder
Alphabet Rock
Sayat Huts 12,500 ft
Cauldron Gap
Easy Valley Col (12,500 ft)
To Panar Laban Huts 11,000 ft
Scale: 5 km 3.1 miles

do some climbing and abseiling, then return, by-passing the hidden half loads, to Panar Laban huts so that the following morning they could collect their half loads at Sayat-Sayat to restore their equipment to a full load before carrying on with the expedition. The four whippets had a discussion and approached the colonel to ask whether, rather than carry half loads, they might carry all their kit and stay the night on the mountain so as to save them the effort of going up and down. Neill agreed. In *SOS*, it is said that both groups carried the same weight. Mayfield was nominated to locate a rock face below the summit upon which the Chinese soldiers could be given last minute practice. After that, he, Brittan, Page and Shearer had the task of moving into Easy Valley col at 2pm on 24 February. Cheung, who had upset Neill over the rations business, was told to wake the team members at 2am with a view to them being on their way by 2.30pm. He spent a worried and restless night.

Next morning the ten set off, six with half loads and four with full loads, the torches on their helmets pointing out the way ahead, up the steep incline. When they reached Sayat-Sayat it was still dark and the four with full loads were in the lead. They left the track and hid their bergens. Whilst they were doing that, Neill and the half loaders went on, past the agreed drop-off point. Mann, a stickler for keeping to what was planned, said to Neill, 'Boss, we are at the huts, are we going to dump our half loads?' 'No', he replied, 'just carry on a little bit'. It proved to be quite a little bit, to just below the summit. It was hard work, particularly with the altitude problem, but it seemed pointless taking packs up a steep track which did not have to be negotiated *en route* to the Gully. All that was achieved was a further weakening of the weak. Mayfield watched this turn of events and the belated off-loading of kit without comment:

> I thought it was a really stupid place to dump the kit: one, because it was so far up the path and two, because they were going to have to carry it back down again and it was a complete waste of time. I later found out the Colonel was trying to increase the group's stamina. Now as far as I am concerned, training should take place before the exercise, not while you are out on the hill.

At 6.15am, all ten members of the team stood, half frozen, on the summit of Mount Kinabalu to watch the rising sun. It was very cold standing up there. For the majority, it proved to be a great anticlimax, surrounded as they were by battalions of Japanese tourists jostling for foot space to view what on that day was an unspectacular sunrise. More attention was devoted to a large rat's efforts to forage for food up on the peak. The influence of altitude affected the strong and less strong alike. Page had already fallen ill along the way, and now Brittan was seen to be suffering alongside Foster, Mann, Cheung and Chow. With the sun now in the ascendancy, the four British non-commissioned officers went off to execute their part of the plan, picking up their bergens on the way. The other six set off to explore the ridges and plateaux and to 'bag' a few peaks. During the course of this exploration, Neill, Foster and Mann went out along a rocky spine from which fell 'a 3,000 ft drop'. It was quite safe up there, but Cheung and Chow hung back. Noticing this, Mann went to talk to them. Cheung took him aside. Mann was a sergeant and the obvious choice to act as intermediary between the Chinese and Neill. Cheung said to Mann, 'none of us wants to carry on'. Mann declined to act as messenger and told Cheung it was no good talking to him. If Cheung and the other two felt that way, they must speak to the Colonel direct. 'He won't bite your heads off. If you really feel that strongly, *you* must do it, it's not for me to do.'

After spending some time at the summit, Neill's group collected their half loads and went down to the rendezvous point beneath the Donkey's Ears to marry up with the other four. By this time Lam was also feeling unwell, so, by the time the three Chinese soldiers arrived for their rock climbing training, they were unable to participate due to illness. Dehydration was as much a cause as the altitude. They were found to be wearing far too much clothing. Neill wrote that he was unable to *persuade* them to take their waterproofs off. The British non-commissioned officers created a *basha* or shelter from a fly sheet, where the Chinese could rest. Two hours later, having had some food and drink, the Chinese soldiers, their strength restored, were ready for instruction. Mayfield took them through a two hour session of rock climbing and abseiling on an exposed but not dangerous face, after which they returned to the Panar Laban Huts having hidden their half loads. Inside the hut, Cheung again approached Mann who reluctantly spoke to the Colonel. He told Neill that the Chinese soldiers did not want to continue, to which he said Neill replied, 'If they want to say anything, Bob, they will have to approach me.'

The four British non-commissioned officers who had stayed out on the slopes collected together their packs and equipment and set off in accordance with their instructions to reconnoitre Easy Valley. The expedition was now split. Mayfield, Brittan, Shearer and Page in the advance group would not come together with the main group comprising Neill, Foster, Cheung, Lam and Chow, for the remainder of the expedition.

Mann, ill at ease, went down to the restaurant. There he met two British soldiers staying at the accommodation, charging the batteries for Major Foster's camera. The soldiers had a large bag of surplus food, principally Gurkha jungle rations which, together with Foster's battery, Mann took back to his group, inviting them to help themselves. He neglected to do so himself and Mayfield, his partner, was already up on the mountain. He went back down to the restaurant for a beer. The two soldiers he had met earlier were still there, also having a beer each. He sat down with them. One gestured to Mann's Commando T-shirt bearing the numbers 383.

'You a booty (marine)?', he asked.

'No,' said Mann, 'logistic corps. What are you two doing up here?' The two explained that they had just been on Brunei Jungle Training and were now enjoying a spot of rest and recuperation before returning to Brunei via Labuan. Mann did not like to ask which regiment they were with.

The other man asked, 'What are you doing on the mountain?' Mann told them of the expedition's aim of beating Low's Gully.

'Have you had any jungle training?'

'Why?', asked Mann, 'We're only going into a gully.' The two soldiers looked at one another silently before one spoke to Mann:

> Bob, I don't know you from Adam, but there are a few important things I should point out. Firstly, you've got three men who don't want to go. Secondly, the group's got no experience whatsoever of the jungle. Thirdly, no one has ever been down there before, and lastly, there are no comprehensive maps of the area. If I were you, I'd go sick.

Mann dismissed their pessimism. 'Nonsense, we'll do the Gully and you can read all about it in the newspapers.'

At 8am on 24 February, Neill led the main body out of the Panar Laban Huts with a view to making the planned rendezvous with the advance group at Easy Valley col at 2pm. The trekkers went past Sayat-Sayat Hut on the tourist track, bearing right towards Easy Valley col and within 1,000 ft of their half loads hidden in the bushes the previous day. With Mann's kit was his 'yellow peril' and he assumed that they would collect it before moving away to the east towards Easy Valley col.

'What about our kit, boss?' Mann asked.

'We'll get it later,' came the reply.

Mann looked at Neill. He looked ill, very weak, not his normal self. His eyes were sunken, he was white under the eyes, his complexion ashen, and his shirt over his head merely complemented a dreadful sight. Aware of Mann's close interest, Neill reprimanded him for not building up the cairns, it being practice in the mountains for trekkers to add a stone to cairns as they passed along the way. 'I'm not a brickie,' mumbled Mann.

As they climbed up to Easy Valley col, with the Chinese interspersed between Neill, Foster and Mann, the latter remained concerned for the safety of his camera and equipment. Gradually Neill fell behind, and Mann and the Chinese arrived at the rendezvous point 45 minutes ahead of schedule. They set about hiding the contents of their rucksacks in the overhang of a cave as a preliminary to going back to recover their half loads.

'Sergeant Mann, what are you doing?' asked Neill when he arrived.

'Preparing to return to pick up our gear,' replied Mann.

'We will go back later,' said Neill.

The advance group had spent the night as planned in Easy Valley. They were up early the next morning in order to find a suitable camp site. It was not long before they were confronted by thickish scrub. However, they persevered and, when they finally broke through, were rewarded with the discovery of a good camp site in which there was a large rock, named Alphabet or Table Rock, and a good supply of water. The rock was called Alphabet Rock by the first group for it was here, while they waited, that they played an alphabet game. Later, when the second group came through, they stopped at the same place, naming it Table Rock. The time taken to hack through the jungle – four hours – meant that in their minds it was now too late for the advance party to get back to the rendezvous point. Mayfield took a large, 5 ft square fluorescent panel out of his bergen and decided that the four of them should sit tight until Neill's group caught them up.

Neill waited at the rendezvous point. In front of them lay a wide panorama, to such an extent that anyone moving towards them could have been seen well in advance of their arrival. Soon after 2pm he decided to move the main body on.

'OK, we're going into the Gully', he declared.

Mann interjected: 'But what about our kit behind us?'

'We'll pick it up later', came the reply. This continuing unwillingness of Neill to share his intentions with his subordinates is indicative of an overall absence of essential communications which, more than any other factor, resulted in the expedition's failure and associated risk to the individuals. Communications are the oxygen of good team work.

Mann walked alongside Foster. 'Is the Colonel all right?' he asked. According to Mann, Foster replied dispassionately: 'He's probably feeling the heat.' They walked for ninety minutes following cairns and sticks until at 3.30pm they stopped for the night in Easy Valley. Neill's concern was to find a supply of drinking water and here, where they intended to camp, they found a small spring. Neill conferred with his deputy, Foster. He was extremely angry that the advance group had not done as instructed and been at the rendezvous point. He discussed the possibility of taking disciplinary action. The leader had just cause to be angry. Mayfield's group had allegedly become stuck, yet here, unlike elsewhere, there were clear, precise orders to be at this given place. However, there was no designated leader in the forward group. Someone, surely, could have been sent back or the group could have got back, had they been so inclined. The Board of Inquiry is said to have commented critically on Neill's action after Mayfield's group had failed to reach the rendezvous point. It is believed to have observed on the absence of urgency to unite the groups or re-establish contact, apparently as though the groups *wished* to remain apart.

There were still a couple of hours of daylight remaining when Neill's group stopped. Foster and Mann went out to reconnoitre the surrounding area. Mann continued along the trail until he reached a steep drop, which he descended. There, against the rock face, he found a note. 'Follow the M1 through the jungle until you come to a dry river bed, then follow the dry river bed.' ('M1' refers to the main route through the jungle.) He did that until he came to the front edge of some 15 ft high scrub where white mining tape denoted a cleared path leading into the heart of the tangled mass. Mann went in until he came to an open patch, from which point the path disappeared. As time was now against him he turned back, rejoining Neill and Foster at 5.15pm. On the way, he had stood on a rock and seen the four non-commissioned officers 2,800 ft distant upon

Alphabet Rock. Foster took up the binoculars and confirmed that they were indeed there.

By the time they returned to the Chinese it was becoming dark. They lit a fire of brushwood collected in the vicinity of the camp site. There was a full moon that night and they could see the mountain slopes around them, but in between there was a band of impenetrable darkness running away from them and narrowing until it disapeared The Gully refused to reveal its secrets. What *was* known was that, between them and the Panataran River, it would be possible to fit Ben Nevis, Britain's highest mountain, two and a half times.

Mann felt the overwhelming sense of spookiness which had beset him on the climb up. He had a restless sleep all night, being woken by a noise in the early hours. Half afraid to open his eyes, he looked out from his sleeping bag to see a large, stumbling, shambling creature moving away from the camp site. Terrified, he spent the rest of the night praying for the reassuring rays of morning. He told Foster what he had seen and heard. Foster confirmed that he too had heard the same noise and seen a shadow outlined against the wall of his tent. He thought it best not to be inquisitive.

The situation facing Neill on the morning of 25 February was that although he had the advance party in his sight, the two groups were separated by a thick band of scrub. To compound his problems further, he still had the half loads out on the ridge above the Sayat-Sayat Huts. He had brought no radios with him and thus was unable either to signify his intentions or pass orders to the advance group. After his rescue, Neill defended his decision not to take radios by saying that they did not work in the Gully. Small section radios would have worked in circumstances where a line of sight or uninterrupted line of communications existed. That much was proven by the RAF Mountain Rescue Team who used hand-held Motorola radios to good effect. Indeed, despite assertions that radios did not work in the Gully, the group had intended to buy hand-held sets in Hong Kong. When the flight schedule prevented that, Neill and Foster sought unsuccessfully to buy radios in Kota Kinabalu.

At 7.30am Neill turned the main group about, to retrace their steps of the previous day to collect their equipment left beyond Sayat-Sayat Hut. This diversion took seven and a half hours. During the course of that diversion, the British built a *basha* in which the Chinese could shelter from the sun while they climbed up to Commando Cauldron to 'bag' the peak and get some video footage. When they came back down they dismantled the *basha* and, together with the Chinese, retraced their steps of that morning. Not until 3pm were they back at the point from whence they had started early that morning. One can now discern the beginnings of a lack of sense of urgency. Neill's concern had been for the Chinese. He said he had not wished to risk Chow with a full load and had to concentrate upon bringing the Chinese down. 'My job,' he said, 'was to balance abilities.' He had not, however, balanced abilities when he had forced the laden Chinese unnecessarily up the track to the peak on the 23rd.

On arrival at the camp site, Mann began repacking his bergen until it was full. Neill, watching him, asked, 'what are you doing?'

'Packing all my kit to move forward, boss,' he replied.

'We're not moving forward tonight, we're moving forward tomorrow,' said Neill.

Mann, totally perplexed, described how he tried to hide his exasperation. Here they were, on a time-critical mission, having consumed two of ten days' rations and now into the third day, without having covered one day's distance. It was still only 3pm. Mann explained that he was not trying to be funny by loading all his kit but that he had to marry up with his tent and Mayfield, his opposite number, and frankly couldn't see any point in walking up and down with half loads. Mann felt fit, becoming stronger every day. Neill saw the wisdom in what he had to say and said that he and Foster would accompany him to recce the route to Alphabet Rock. Mann carried his full load, the other two half loads.

They turned into the pathway where the undergrowth had been marked by white mine-laying tape. Standing in the clearing from which there was no obvious exit, Neill and Foster indicated that they would have to get back before dark. It was now about 4.30pm. They left their half loads there, on the ground, with Mann's 'yellow peril'. Mann set off by himself in the direction of Alphabet Rock. The four on the rock could hear him crashing about and they began shouting to him. They could hear Mann shouting back but, after a while, they noticed a change in his voice to one of acute anxiety. It dawned upon them that he was alone.

'Who's there with you, Bob?'

'Just me,' came the reply.

Pushing onward, he took the line of least resistance, which also took him off in a westerly direction. Suddenly, there was nothing in

1. New's Pools in the dry season. (*Robert New*)

2. Robert New and Steve Pinfield in Low's Gully. (*Robert New*)

3. The tourist track leading up to the peak of Mount Kinabalu. (*Sabah Parks*)

4. Eric Wong, Head Warden of Kinabalu National Park. (*R M Connaughton*)

5. Major General John Foley, Commander British Forces Hong Kong, and Brigadier General Hussin Mohammed Yussoff, Fifth Brigade commander. (*Borneo Mail*)

6. Lieutenant Commander Cliff Williams and Lieutenant Colonel Tony Schumacher. (*Borneo Mail*)

7. Lumpiol's house where Mann and Mayfield were taken for food, treatment and rest. (*Borneo Mail*)

8. Two members of the RAF Mountain Rescue Team returning to their base, 17 March 1994. (*Borneo Mail*)

9. Captain Izhar Hassan. (*Borneo Mail*)

10. Flight Lieutenant Gabriel Joel. (*Borneo Mail*)

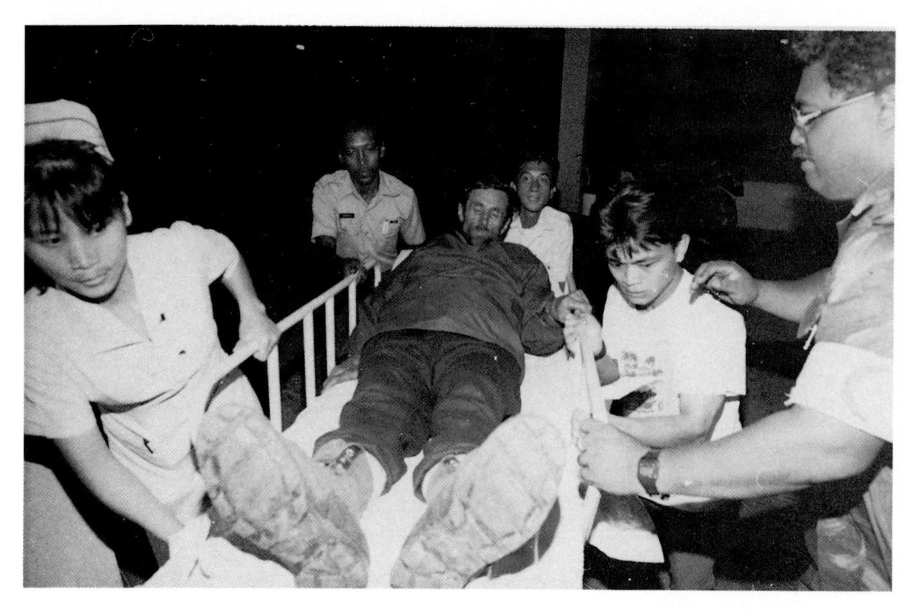

11. Neill being stretchered into the Sabah Medical Centre. (*Borneo Mail*)

12. Cheung after the rescue. (*Borneo Mail*)

13. Foster, having left the rescue helicopter, is seen here with Lieutenant Colonel Schumacher. (*Borneo Mail*)

14. All smiles at the York Press Conference. L–r Neill, Brittan and Foster. (*The Press Agency*)

15. Mayfield and Mann in Low's Gully. (*Bob Mann*)

'Author of jungle trip book in row on accuracy'
– the headline of the *Western Morning News* on 15 May 1995 which accompanied this picture of Mayfield confronting Foster at a signing of Neill and Foster's book, *SOS*, in a Plymouth bookshop. (*Western Morning News*)

front of him as he stood, teetering, on the brink of a 300-foot drop. The four all saw him at the same time. 'Stay there!', shouted Mayfield, who brought him safely to Alphabet Rock.

Neill and Foster returned, unencumbered, to the camp site where they had left the Chinese. The need to reassure the Chinese soldiers is perfectly understandable, but what the two leaders had done by both returning to their former camp site was to miss the opportunity of restoring communications between the two groups. But then, unlike Mann, they had only taken forward half their individual loads, the remainder having been left with the Chinese. Mann's incentive to change groups was compelling. He had carried forward a full load and had thereby put himself in a position so to do. Mann had been given permission to press on but maintained that he had been given no instructions whatsoever other than the authority to join up with the advance group. Neill, who by this time was being affected and discomfited by what was clearly a viral infection, could not recall having given Mann any particular orders. Foster, however, had a notion that Mann's instructions were to remain with the advance party at Alphabet Rock or face the consequences of a veiled threat that he would have to chaperone the Chinese soldiers for the remainder of the exercise.

Meanwhile, at Alphabet Rock, Brittan, Page and Shearer had been kicking their heels, waiting for the main group to catch up with them. Mayfield had gone off early that morning to check out their onward route. He returned at midday to find only the other three members of his group, and no one else. By now, all four were extremely irritated by their lack of progress. They had come all this way to do something no one else had previously achieved and were supremely confident in their ability to conquer Low's Gully. But, for the time being, here they were, sitting on the side of a mountain, inactive, frustrated, bored, and eating the limited amount of food they would need to sustain them as they progressed through the Gully.

Hopes were raised when at 6pm Mann made his appearance, only to be dashed when it was confirmed that he was alone. Since he had no instructions for them, all he could do was to recount what the main group had done since the two groups separated. As Mann spoke, what became the source of Group A's continuing frustration was his account of Group B's movements being conducted in half load shuttles. 'I've been marching up and down like the f. . .ing grand old Duke of York,' said Mann. As they chuntered among themselves, the non-commissioned officers agreed that a far better ploy would be to take full loads slowly. Bearing in mind the distance to be covered down the Gully, the whippets formed the opinion that the half load business, if it were to continue, would not enable them to achieve their goal. Mann said that, since he would have to go back to retrieve the 'yellow peril', he would go on and meet the colonel, explain the route, and tell him what the others had been doing. He understood the need to restore communications.

There is no doubt at all that the concept of Social Darwinism expressed earlier was now widely abroad among Group A. One of them admitted, 'We were just looking for the excuse to push on.' In his book, Neill makes an oblique reference to Captain Queeg of the *Caine Mutiny*. There was no mutiny here but there was a widening of the division created on Day 1. Foster was right in maintaining that they were impatient to get on, but the cause of the division in the first place was due to the leadership's failure to exert the necessary command and control. The non-commissioned officers were doing what they do best – getting on and doing what they had come to do without an excess of analysis or thought. With Mann now in the advance group, the groups each comprised five men, so it would be appropriate to describe the former advance group of British non-commissioned officers as Group A and the former main group comprising the two officers and the Chinese soldiers as Group B. David Powell was to say later that if Neill had set out with Group A at the outset having sent back the Chinese soldiers as requested, together with Foster, there was a prospect of them succeeding. Powell remained critical of what they had intended to do. He told the Board of Inquiry as much. Neill challenged him, as he had earlier: 'You have never been in the Gully.' To which Powell replied: 'You have only got to look over the edge into the abyss to comprehend what the difficulties are.'

4
Disintegration

Early on the morning of the 26th, Mann headed up through the strip of jungle, using a machete to widen the track and marking it with white mine-laying tape. He passed the point where the luggage lay and continued on to Group B's camp site. Neill appeared confused and was unable to remember approving Mann's journey forward to make contact with Group A. He had spent a restless night and so inflamed was his throat that he could barely communicate. He sat there drinking tea while they talked. Foster was not present, he had gone off to find water. Mann explained to the team leader what Group A had achieved in the meantime, and asked permission for that group to go further down towards the Gully, to Lone Tree, where Mayfield had set up a point from which to abseil. To save time, Mann suggested that Group A be permitted to go down that abseil to the fringe of the jungle, where they could cut a path in preparation for the arrival of Group B. Mann told the author that Neill had said to him: 'Yes Bob, no problem at all, it will be good to resume communications with the first group. See you later.' Mann prepared to leave at 9am, taking with him, as he believed, permission for Group A to proceed as he had suggested. At the end of his conversation with the colonel, Foster appeared, but did not ask what had been going on. That was the last Mann saw of both of them for the duration of the exercise. He picked up the 'yellow peril' at 10am and brought to the expectant Group A the news they had been waiting for: to proceed to the next stage and wait there.

Without any hesitation, they moved immediately to Mayfield's abseil point at Lone Tree to descend some 160 feet. After another stretch of hacking through undergrowth, they came to a shorter abseil of 40 feet. It was now 2pm and the non-commissioned officers decided to establish camp at the foot of the abseil while Mayfield went off to reconnoitre.

What Mayfield's reconnaissance revealed was a further three abseils, which he believed would take the Group down to the floor of Low's Gully. Thus, this total of five abseils was more than twice as many as those done by New and Pinfield during the course of their exploration of the Gully. The two civilians' philosophy of travelling light and fast meant that they often scrambled down slopes which the soldiers, owing to the heaviness of their bergens, were obliged to abseil. In the Gully, however, a variation of 16 feet to the left or right opened up a whole set of different problems. But Mayfield's group did not follow New's and Pinfield's route so that, in terms of measurement, the number of abseils was not a valid comparison. Nevertheless, what New and Pinfield had done was never far from Group A's thoughts. It served as a telling yardstick.

After four days, the whippets had achieved only marginally more than New and Pinfield had achieved in one. Worst of all, they had consumed four of their ten days' rations. To the astute, fit and able young non-commissioned officers, it seemed that the only way they could achieve their mission was to accelerate the action, yet there was always the consideration of Group B, now established in their minds as a millstone round their necks. By nightfall there was still no news of Group B, so Mayfield decided that in the morning he would make his way back to meet them to receive further instructions.

Meanwhile, Group B had departed their camp site close on the heels of Mann. The path to what they called Table Rock (called Alphabet Rock by Group A) was by now clearly evident and, after walking for two hours, they arrived there at 11am. Foster was shocked and angry that Group A had gone on ahead without waiting. He did not know that Neill had given them permission to proceed. This burgeoning antagonism was common to both groups. By now, Neill's illness had taken hold. Any judgements regarding what Neill did or did not do have to be tempered by the recognition of the effect this enervating sickness had upon his decision-making processes and his energy. The Colonel admits that he was out of action for a good day, unable to recall accurately his conversations with either Mann or Mayfield. He was clearly very ill, virtually unable to walk, and had lost his voice. Foster arranged for Neill to be placed in the shade in his sleeping bag, where he was to rest until the next day. Foster took over as expedition commander and sent out Cheung and Lam to find

Group A's abseil point and leave a message there for them. Cheung and Lam searched the area where they believed the point of descent should have been, but to no avail. Instead, they left the message on Group A's dive sacks, close to the distinctive House Boulder, before returning with the news that they had encountered no one. That afternoon, Foster took Chow with him to collect the equipment which he and Neill had dumped the night before.

The next morning, the 27th, Foster was up early to leave at 6.15am for House Boulder, where he exchanged notes. The new one gave Group A revised instructions to make rendezvous there at 11am. Meanwhile at House Boulder, Foster searched for an abseil point and expressed surprise at finding one. He knew that New and Pinfield had scrambled down here on their backsides. Mayfield had been obliged to put an abseil here because, with their heavy packs, the novices certainly could not have negotiated the 160 ft (50 m) drop without a rope. The implications of that rope were profound. Its presence should have trumpeted a loud warning that the earlier time and space appreciation should be urgently reassessed.

On his way back to Table Rock, Mayfield saw an apparently much recovered Neill not only standing on the rock but using his restored voice to shout out to Foster that Mayfield was working his way up to Table Rock. Standing on the rock, looking down the valley, Neill watched Mayfield climbing up in his running kit towards him to his right, while to his left, separated by perhaps 300 ft, was Foster. Mayfield had left his group at 8am and climbed back up the two ropes he had left in place for Group B to use. Surprised at first to find Group B not at House Boulder, he found instead the note Foster had left there that morning. On his way up, Mayfield passed close to Foster, who told him that Neill had been unwell. Very soon, Mayfield identified Neill standing on Table Rock and made his way up to join him. He had no idea that Neill had been out of action and had chosen not to linger with Foster.

Mayfield did not find Neill very different from usual. Their meeting was perfectly amicable, Neill giving Mayfield a cup of tea. Admittedly he did seem a touch below par, but otherwise he was much himself, with full control of his voice. Mayfield was taken aback that the Colonel seemed 'in no rush at all' as he sat down to drink his tea. He found the Chinese to be in good spirits. Mayfield and Neill stayed together on the rock, where they engaged in conversation for 20 minutes. Mayfield outlined what they had done and explained the two sets of abseils – the first set of two, and the second set of three. He said that, in his opinion, after the last abseil in the second set, a descent of 180 ft, they would be on the floor of Low's Gully. Mayfield anticipated that they could all reach that point by the evening. He accordingly sought permission to go down to what he then believed to be the floor of Low's Gully. Mayfield explained to Neill that, due to the unexpected number and length of abseils they had encountered, he would have to pull his ropes through. *This meant that his group could not get back up the valley.* He promised, however, to leave the belays in position, to which Neill's group could attach their own ropes.

Neill apparently agreed, and told Mayfield to crack on and clear a path and make rendezvous with him that evening at the bottom of the abseils. Mayfield mentioned to Neill the serious situation regarding rations, which meant that Group A could only reasonably linger on the floor of Low's Gully until early on the morning of 28 February. Mayfield said to Neill that if he was not there, Group A had no option but to push on. 'I am afraid, boss, that I cannot wait longer than the next morning.' At the Board of Inquiry, Neill contested what Mayfield alleged he had said, emphasising that he would never have tolerated such arrogance. Although the leader's and rock climbing expert's versions were never to be reconciled, the Board found in favour of Mayfield's judgement. Brittan said:

> I was always convinced that Neill would look at the array of obstacles ahead of him and shy away. Due to the developing problem with our rations, what we were in effect saying to our leader was 'get down and meet with us or we shall be obliged to move on'. We couldn't just sit there and starve. We were committed. We had no choice.

After talking to Neill, Mayfield then talked to Foster. It is more than a little curious that Mayfield had these two distinctly separate conversations. After appearing out of the bush following a significant period of absence of five days, it might have been expected that Foster would wish to join in the discussion with Neill to find out what was going on. Foster had, after all, assumed command of the expedition, a position he held for 36 critical hours. Foster repeated that Neill had been ill and was having what he described as 'mood swings', but the fact that Foster had assumed command was not related to Mayfield. They then rehearsed much of the earlier discussion Neill had had with Mayfield regarding the abseils and the route ahead. Foster reckoned that his group could reach the top of the second set of abseils by 11.30am. Taking with him two additional ropes and Group B's two *parangs* (machetes used for cutting undergrowth), Mayfield took his leave of Group B, rejoining his own group at 10.30am. Why they did not all go together is not clear, but it seems indicative of the emergent independence of the two groups. It is also a fact that despite being mid-morning, Neill's group had not struck camp, something that would require another hour. If the dissent which had bubbled over in the hut at the outset of the exercise was the first nail in the expedition's coffin, what did *not* happen here was most assuredly the second, because it was the last stage at which the exercise might have been saved. Mayfield needed precise orders to 'wait where you are until we arrive', or 'reassemble your group back on us'. If, due to his disability, Neill was unable to do this, why did Foster not exert himself?

The indisposition of the leader and the breakdown or absence of leadership for 36 hours begs the question of the role and function of the deputy leader. Was Foster, fat and well over 50, ever intended to lead? Or was he a prop to support the remote and distant Neill, a familiar face among the unfamiliar? He did not hold the respect of the young British element. From what position was it intended he should lead? If Neill was hoping to make a serious attempt on Low's Gully then past friendships should have been set aside.

There were mixed thoughts among the four non-commissioned officers awaiting Mayfield's reappearance after his interview with the Colonel. Brittan was raring to go, 'my mind was already at the bottom of the Gully, it was just a case of getting my body to catch up with it,' but Mann had private thoughts that, in view of the difficulties encountered thus far and those looming ahead, the expedition would be called off. When Mayfield appeared at 10.30am, he briefed the others:

> We have permission to continue to the bottom of the abseils and to wait there. We will wait there a reasonable amount of time, then we will have to push on.
>
> 'What?', said Mann, 'he still wants us to carry on?'
>
> 'Yes', replied Mayfield.
>
> 'How far behind is the Colonel?', asked Mann.

Mayfield replied:

> I've climbed two ropes and walked to the Colonel ... It's taken me

> three-quarters of an hour. At worst they're two hours behind, so we'll probably see them tonight. All the belay points are in place.

They began the first of the three abseils, 160 ft, at 11am. Going over the edge proved frightening. 'If you'd slipped', said Mayfield, 'you would have gone all the way'. Progressively they all completed the third and, once into the jungle at the bottom, found, to their horror, that the floor of the Gully was still a considerable way below them. Despite his illness, Neill is quite clear in his own mind that he and Mayfield understood that the rendezvous should occur after this, the third, abseil had taken Mayfield's group to the edge of the jungle which they could see. Mayfield had miscalculated. He was used to climbing in a European environment where it was routine to gauge height by comparison against known objects, cars or trees. But now, in the Gully, among strange and unfamiliar vegetation, he was unable to judge how far away objects were. Calculated judgements had given way to sheer guesswork. He had no other option but to throw a rope over a cliff and see where it landed.

In fact they had to undertake an additional six abseils down 900 ft before definitely reaching the bottom of the Gully after 5pm. This did not augur at all well for the rejoining of the groups. Group B, short on physical fitness and experience, had conditioned itself to completing its immediate task after five abseils. Unbeknown to them, that was less than half of the requirement. Moreover, there were no contingency plans to cater for such an unexpected development. Group A pondered the predicament of those above them. They lit a large bonfire to signify that they had descended deeper into the Gully. This unavoidable fact they had reinforced along their way by means of cairns of stones, fixed belay points, marks, and written messages along the course of their descent. Brittan had been the author of a number of jocular written messages. One read:

> Congratulations. You are now half way to getting wet! Don't forget to pull the ropes through. See you at the bottom for tea and toast. The advance party wishes you a pleasant journey. Keep smiling.

He had not signed the message but had drawn at the bottom of the page the outline of the parachute wings, which contained its own, unspoken message. Brittan insisted that his little messages were never intended to be provocative. 'I always write messages like that, including the parachute wings. They are intended to be jovial,' he said. Significantly, Group A had passed their committing moment. They could not climb back out of the Gully the way they had come, for they had neither the equipment nor the ability.

Group B arrived at Boulder Rock at 11am. They picked up their equipment and tackled the first set of abseils. Progress was slow, for Neill rightly insisted that the Chinese should go down on a safety rope. Now they were paying the penalty of not having instituted a training programme for the Chinese and insisting that they were trained to a high standard before the UK and Hong Kong groups made rendezvous. The progress on those first abseils resembled that of a novice familiarisation session. All the time, the clock was ticking. They negotiated the first two abseils and had completed the first abseil in the set of three when the rope became stuck. Still weak from his illness, Neill did not have the strength to climb up the rope to release it, nor was he prepared to delegate the task to his deputy or the novices, even though it was arguably well within Cheung's capabilities. Why Foster had not gone for it is also unclear. When comparing himself with his younger brother Bernard, Foster had described him as *'another experienced climber and hill-walker'*. Accordingly, at 3.30pm they called it a day and prepared their camp for the night, out on a ledge below the snared rope. Time being wasted was now accumulating. Neill calculated that he was still within New's schedule.

Obviously Group A was oblivious of this further, unfortunate development. They had now been quite seriously slowed down by Group B, to the extent that the point they had now reached, after five days, was where New and Pinfield were after only a day and a half. As each day passed, so too did the food situation worsen. They were unaware of just how bad the food situation had become. Overly confident of their own abilities, they were still consuming one ration per day, in the belief that it would come out all right in the end. They had not yet reached New's Pools and, if they had to take the escape route to the east, they would need three to four days' rations, which was exactly what they had in their packs at that very moment.

Group harmony remained good as they discussed these and other issues. They made good progress hopping down over rocks, sometimes plunging into the water. Mayfield allowed the group a free hand to negotiate the obstacles in their own way, to extemporise, something he would not have done had Neill been there. Leadership here was based upon ability in the environment facing them. To that extent, rank had gone into the melting pot. By their judgement, they concluded that they had no option but to press on. They scanned with binoculars the rock faces rising above them, for signs of Group B. Once, and only once, two days later, did they see someone without a bergen (and, by implication, his group), whom they estimated to be a day or more away. They would also have been aware that Group B might not yet have passed its committing point, so in their minds there was a real possibility that the person they had seen, believed to have been Foster, was on his way up and out rather than continuing with the descent. In view of the difficulties encountered thus far, a withdrawal of Group B might not have seemed to be an irrational decision. The five came to a group decision that, since they were now down to four full days' rations, there was no point in sitting where they were if, indeed, Neill had gone back up the Gully. They decided to carry on, but still to leave messages and build cairns.

When Group B awoke on the morning of 28 February, it was judgement day for the leader. If Neill hauled down the rope which had become caught up the previous afternoon, then that would put the team beyond their committing point, the point of no return and the unequivocal commitment of going down into Low's Gully. Pulling that rope down really had to be thought through because of its very serious implications, a matter of life or death. Neill and Foster had no reason to believe that they could not still achieve what they had set out to do.

In fact for Neill the leader, there was little option. It is possible to question Neill's judgement, yet he most assuredly demonstrated that leadership does not come without responsibility. Arguably he could have come to no other conclusion than to press on, to regain control of the advance group and lead it out of potential difficulty. But he could not go on alone, nor could he send the Chinese back unaccompanied by either himself or Foster. Neill climbed the rope and freed it. Now, all ten spiders were in the bath. The only escape was down the plug hole. The laborious process of encouraging the novices down the rock faces continued. All the while, time was being lost, and this was serious because they had the same problem with rations as Group A. When the group eventually reached what Mayfield had led them to believe was the bottom of the Gully, they had to brace themselves for a further six abseils. By this time, Group A had moved over half a mile further down the valley, thereby increasing the time separation between the two groups to 48 hours.

Neill said there had never been any question of turning back. Mayfield had no maps and a decreasing supply of stores. The Colonel had arranged to hand over the reserve climbing kit to Mayfield at the rendezvous point. Most of Cheung's kit was with Shearer, and the Chinese were becoming more and more proficient. 'It never occurred to me for one moment that they would not be there,' said Neill who, from the outset, had been conditioned to believe he had only two abseils to complete. Even when this proved to be overly optimistic, he and Mayfield had both thought they could see the bed of the Gully from their earlier observation point. However, it was a false crest with plenty of depth beyond. A point to ponder is that perhaps Neill was still unaware of what really lay ahead. Soon, it would become crystal clear. There is sometimes a 'chopper' mentality associated with the taking of risks, the supposition being that if the situation really gets bad, a helicopter will pluck those in difficulty out.

The rain began to fall at 3pm on 1 March. The stream that had been making its rather languid progress downhill perceptibly gathered momentum, spreading beyond its original confines, becoming a raging torrent in a short space of time. Rocks which had once been dry and safe stepping stones had now become wet, slippery and extremely dangerous. Group A sought out shelter, which they found in the area later to be known as Kevin's Cave, where they settled for the night.

The next morning they struck out for New's Pools, which they reached at noon on 2 March. They stood there, as New and Pinfield had before them, contemplating their situation. The pools were 8–9 feet wide and approximately 30–40 feet long. At the time, they were more concerned with what lay ahead. There was obviously no way out up the sides. They reflected upon the possibility of jumping into the pools and swimming across. The big question was, however, what then? Their first thoughts were to continue into the Gully rather than seek out New's escape route, which lay to their right. By now, the water flowing downhill had become fast and wild, channelled into a gorge no more than 25 ft wide, and from which there rose vertical, smooth, granite walls a few hundred feet high. Their second thoughts were that to go down that path would be insane. From their briefings, however, they knew that the path to their right, assuming they found it, would take them out of the Gully. The implication being that if they took it, their mission to conquer Low's Gully would fail. They decided to go left, or westward, to seek out a satisfactory route to bypass the obstacle ahead of them and bring them back on line just below it. They spent a miserably uncomfortable night perched on a narrow ledge thirty feet above the now thundering waterfalls emptying into New's Pools. All the while, the torrential rain pelted down to the degree that they were unable to go on. This particular jungle was not neutral; it was positively against them, providing them with nothing with which to bolster their declining food stocks. Brittan said that for the duration of the expedition he saw two snakes the size of pencils and three raspberries. That night, the morale of that sodden group had reached rock bottom.

Soaked and dispirited, the group followed Mayfield across a number of treacherous rock faces. When they turned the corner, having by-passed New's Pools, they were confronted by a lost world. They had reached an entirely new zone of difficulty. The going became progressively worse, the terrain harder and the ration stocks declined. The skyscraper-sized waterfalls and bottomless pools dictated a regime of swimming, walking and scrambling. All thoughts of Neill and his people simply evaporated as they struggled to cope with their own, acute problems. Their humour had not been best served by having to climb up almost 400 ft, hauling their heavy, wet bergens behind them. The rain had not abated. Not only had their morale flagged, but now their energy was also ebbing away from them as if carried away on the floods which surrounded them. Much of their time was spent on all fours, cutting their way through the jungle.

Mayfield had led because, as the technician, the expert rock climber, he held sway over the rest, dependent as they were upon his expertise and advice. Twice Shearer had dropped his bergen into the water. More than a little annoyed with him after the second time, Mayfield told him to abseil down and collect it. Shearer, doubting his own abilities, pleaded with Mayfield for him to go down and recover the bergen. It was now dusk, the team's confidence and fitness were on the wane. Mayfield resisted Shearer's entreaties: 'You dropped the f. . .ing thing, you go down and get it.'

Once down, Shearer was unable to climb back up with his sodden bergen. By this time he was scared, very cold, and panicking. Mayfield had no option but to set up a hoist and, using the others as a belay, they spent the best part of an hour hauling Shearer up from the river. But now Mayfield was showing the first signs of flagging, having been worn down by the continuous and unavoidable effort and responsibility. The constant need to go off alone and reconnoitre, go down cliffs and come up so often when there was found to be no way through, had contributed to his exhaustion. Then he returned to the group, who had themselves rested, to move on without having rested himself. His climbing experience and leadership had saved the group. Without him they would not have had the skill to negotiate the steep, slimy rock faces. It was at this point that Brittan, Mayfield's senior and physically the stronger of the two, with Mayfield's encouragement gradually took up the leadership. The group spent another desperate and scary night out on a ledge and agreed, by the usual manner of group consensus, to move back towards the direction of the river. This was easier said than done. The rocks and rock faces had been drenched by the continuing tropical downpour and were extremely hazardous. The group negotiated the dangerous waterfalls dressed only in T-shirts, shorts and trainers, and crossed the deep pools by throwing their kit in and swimming after it. On the way down they tried now to keep to the right of the river, convinced that the mountainside was the wrong side from which to escape.

Early on 4 March they picked themselves up and prepared to abseil down a cliff face to bring them level with the river. It was whilst in the process of this two-pitch abseil that a tree which had featured in the abseil gave way. Shearer had been the last to reach the tree and was pulling the abseil rope through when the tree came away from the cliff. Those below watched in horror as, 60 feet above, as if in slow motion, he began to slip. There was a shout as he fell, vertically at first, until his feet became ensnared by vines, turning him round and over, through 180 degrees. He landed half way down on his back, bounced, and described two somersaults before landing, face down, five feet from where an aghast Mayfield stood on a large boulder. 'Casualty', shouted Mayfield at the top of his voice, and rushed to tend to Shearer. Mayfield feared the worst, half expecting to find exposed, shattered bones and brains. He eased Shearer's bergen off and was relieved to find he was coming round. There was a large gash to Shearer's head, he was having difficulty breathing and his legs had been badly bashed by the fall. But fortunately, or so Mayfield thought, there were no bits sticking out that should not have been sticking out. The fall had affected Mayfield in a different way from Shearer. He had found himself frozen by the incident. His brain asked him the question: what would he have done if Shearer had been badly injured or even dying? They could not take him out. His mind considered the options, of killing him and leaving him . . . Mayfield shook himself out of that thought pattern, surprised at his own irrationality but still nonetheless wondering whether it had been so irrational.

It was at this point that Mayfield ceased to function properly. He was clearly affected by the accident, shocked and stunned into inactivity. He was then aware of being thrust aside as Brittan rendered first aid to Shearer. Mayfield drifted off, turned his back on Shearer and began coiling ropes. Brittan reassured Mayfield that Shearer was OK. Being OK was a relative condition, for Shearer was obviously in much pain as they stumbled off towards the Gully. The others ensured that he carried his bergen as they resumed their dangerous boulder hopping down the Gully. The shock of that fall, the sickening sound of a body striking the rocks below, reverberated throughout the group. It was a sobering moment because they were all struck by the fact that if any one of them was to be badly injured, there could be no way out.

Shearer's qualification as a Joint Service Mountain Expedition Leader was one of the two key qualifications necessary to permit the expedition to attempt Low's Gully. But now Shearer could barely walk and was showing signs of concussion. Better to be safe than sorry, they abandoned any further forward progress that day. The night was spent belayed to the rocks some 200 ft above the river. Up there, in the still of the jungle, Page reflected: 'Isn't the army stupid. You do things like this and look what happens.'

On the higher reaches of the Gully there had not been so much as a jungle, but rather scrub upon rock. It was a poor form of jungle in which creepers and waitawhile bushes were prevalent. The latter have long tendrils along which are reverse hooks which, when they snag clothing, require the individual to pause in order to release himself. Overall, however, the main problems at the top were the rocks and the steepness of the terrain. Up there it was of course cold, and up on the peak the group said they found ice. As they descended it became warmer, but not really warm until they reached their respective *kampongs* (villages) at approximately 2,500 ft. The weather pattern began with a bright day, giving way to mist, then rain in the afternoon. The nights began dry but, as the journey went on, the rain continued into the evening. They were not greatly troubled by leeches, black fly and fire ants until towards the end. Shearer's bad leg, however, was particularly affected by leeches. But in the main these ghastly little creatures became more threatening at night when they sought out the body's orifices. The thread leech, which homes-in on the brain, is particularly dangerous. The real jungle was at the lower altitude, and this was where the mosquitoes were much in evidence. Despite having been a scrupulous taker of Paludrine and Chloroquine, Brittan contracted malaria, as did Mayfield and Mann whose anti-malarial tablets were lost along the way. Additionally, their cycle of protection was interrupted because of a warning from a local expert not to use anti-malarial medicines at high altitude.

The next morning, 5 March, the group readdressed the outstanding abseil, a none too easy descent of 200 ft down to the river. Once safely down, they continued along the river until confronted by another impassable waterfall. Mann, the expedition's official video operator, did some filming around the pools where they had stopped. He talked into the camera as he panned around the scene and, as he spoke, he and the others were aware that his tone and his words were performing their requiem. Emotion was not far below the surface of this wiry little West Countryman. He put his camera on a rock and spoke directly into it as though to his wife, apologising for getting himself into this situation. He was clearly deeply moved by what he was doing.

Mayfield climbed up to the jungle line and put a rope down from the ridge. Up there they found *parang* marks and naïvely believed this to be a God-given escape route leading in an easterly direction to an M1 jungle trail. But the ridge just went up, and up, and up. They spent the rest of the day moving along the track until, at approximately 5pm, they came to a narrow clearing up on the ridge which would pass as a camp site for the night. The group members were now suffering their own, individual difficulties. Shearer's fall had obviously shaken him up, so much so that he now found it difficult to keep up with the remainder of the group. He was showing signs of confusion and disorientation. He pleaded to be left behind, to be picked up by a helicopter which, despite the utter impossibility of such a prospect, he seriously believed would come and rescue him. The remainder had urged him on, but noted with concern the swelling of his legs, and his behaviour which was now becoming irrational.

The trail upon which they decided to camp for the night was too narrow to accommodate all five. Mayfield and Mann went back down the track for 100 ft and set up some overhead cover using a flysheet as an awning. Half an hour later the heavens opened, rain pelting down 'like nothing on earth'. The two marines of sorts, both Arctic trained, sat huddled together in the flooded, dripping jungle, the wood too wet to light and their food supply already exhausted. Then a soaked apparition came down the so-called track towards them. It was Brittan. 'We've had a whip round. We've got you something to eat', he explained, handing over lamb granules, dried peas and a packet of soup. Embarrassed yet extremely grateful the two got out their cooker, only to find to their dismay that its seal was about to give out. Fortunately, it lasted long enough to provide the famished pair with what one described as 'the best meal I ever had'. The gift had been so unexpected, but they knew that if the situation had been reversed, they would have done the same. The food situation was now really desperate. Mayfield and Mann were suffering the consequences of having bailed out the Chinese. Brittan had carried in excess of 10 days' rations but he had already drawn on the reserves by helping Shearer. In four days of physically demanding activity, the group had covered at best one mile. They would rue their earlier profligacy with food. Further up the Gully, the Colonel had halved his moribund team's rations and then halved them again.

Mayfield and Mann settled down to a rough night, waking early, cold and wet. They talked in their sleeping bags for half an hour before rising earlier than usual. During the course of their discussion, they decided upon the strategy of the day: to follow the ridge until it hit the main hunters' trail which they believed to be out there somewhere. They were still optimistic, certain that they would get out that day or the next. They had a giggle among themselves about the prospect of telling their grandchildren of the two days in the jungle when they had gone without food. They then looked at their kit – what was really essential? First to be ditched were the helmets, followed by the tent inner, pegs, poles, shirts, trainers and trousers. The President of the Board of Inquiry asked Mann why he had abandoned government property and yet kept his video equipment. Mann thought the reason rather obvious but found difficulty in putting it in so many words before the Board.

Cold and wet, Mayfield and Mann walked along the track to join the other three. They were not in such an advanced state of preparedness. Mann and Mayfield, unwilling to sit and watch the others eat, decided to make an early start. The agreement was that they should wait for the others to catch up when they reached the first track junction. In the jungle, however, it is so easy to lose a track and pick up another. The two marines, Mann and Mayfield picked up their packs and continued their journey down the track while the other three finished their breakfast. After clearing up, Brittan, Page and Shearer followed on, some thirty minutes behind Mann and Mayfield who had set off in an easterly direction and then north over a tributary of the Panataran River. Mann shouted back and heard Page reply, but Brittan's group never caught up with Mann and Mayfield, who by then had gone off on a divergent track. The three following on shouted and whistled, but to no avail. It had not been a malicious break. However, Brittan wondered whether the other two had genuinely become lost or had made a runner, leaving him with an injured man and Page who, to all intents and purposes, was still a novice.*

That night, Brittan's group camped on a track junction and, on the morning of the 7th, turned around to retrace their steps to where they had moved away from the river the previous day. They crossed over the river and headed westward, something which they continued to do for the next four days.

The system Brittan's group developed to move down the numerous waterfalls along their way was to throw their bergens into the water and, once they had floated to the surface, to jump in after them and make for the side of the pool. The only food they had left was some curry powder, cough lozenges and vitamin tablets. Leeches clung to their bodies, making their own contribution towards burning up the men's energy. To add to Shearer's problems, he now had the head of a leech embedded in an eyelid. Half blind and with legs of jelly, he was cajoled forward by Brittan. Brittan still carried his bergen and he expected no less of Shearer, with whom he had less good a rapport than he had with Page. Page had lost his bergen higher up the Gully and had also had a bad fall. He is shorter than Shearer and was also physically weak, but arguably they could have shared the chore of carrying the bergen between them.

---

*This opinion formed part of the testimony Brittan gave at the time of his debriefing. All the soldiers' testimonies were freely distributed among the expedition participants during the course of the Board of Inquiry. The marines were outraged at what Brittan had suggested. The soldiers asked for copies of the two officers' testimonies but were told there were none – the officers apparently had not been debriefed. Since the function of debriefing was to glean information likely to assist in the rescue of Neill's group, this was understandable.

Each waterfall they encountered posed its own specific challenge. Brittan followed the usual procedure of tossing down his bergen into the pool and, once it surfaced, jumping off the cliffs after it, to show the other two that it was possible. On one occasion, after Brittan's bergen had been thrown in, it did not reappear. He was more annoyed than distressed for his food had long gone. Whilst examining the scene to see where his pack had gone, he slipped and tumbled into the pool down a water chute. As soon as he hit the water he was seized in a whirlpool, taken under a large boulder and thrown up into a dark cave. He climbed out of the cave, with his bergen, through a blow hole in the roof, and made his way downstream to reveal himself to the other two who had been following on some way behind. Assuming a normal situation, Shearer jumped in, watched by Page. When Page saw that Shearer had not surfaced he was greatly concerned. Brittan shouted to him from downstream that there really was no problem. Unconvinced, but with no other option, Page jumped in. He had never been a strong swimmer and was totally unprepared for what happened to him. Needless to say, he was mightily relieved to be deposited eventually in the cave. Page and Shearer stood there, looking up at the blow hole. They had difficulty getting Shearer's bergen through the hole and had to unpack each item. Once Brittan returned to lend a hand, they looked for somewhere to sleep for the night because it was becoming dark. For that reason they had little option but to camp where they were, despite the obvious presence of countless leeches. For two days they continued onward, out of food and with very little residual energy.

On 11 March, they came across the first signs of civilisation. Alongside a stream some concreting had been done in preparation for the building of a small power station. Then, lo and behold, the three starved soldiers emerged into a banana plantation, the trees laden with ripe fruit. There was an instinctive move towards the fruit, only to be halted by Brittan. 'What are you doing? That's stealing. This is a Muslim country, don't you know you can get your arms cut off for stealing?' The other two took him at his exaggerated word and stumbled on. Then, suddenly, on a tractor they saw an old man. He offered them what they took to be a rudimentary cigarette but, not being confident as to exactly what the loose-packed stuff between the paper was, they declined. The old Malaysian could not speak English but, from his pointing, they understood where they had to go.

Eventually they emerged at the village of Melangkap Tamis in the late afternoon of 11 March 1994.

When they arrived in the village there were some children playing football. The game stopped abruptly as villagers from all corners converged upon the three apparitions which had arrived among them. They were gaunt and haggard, their clothes in tatters, and their visible skin torn to shreds. The village schoolteacher, Mr Yapis Juriba, came forward and guided them into his house. He could see they were close to starvation. Reassuring them in impeccable English, he prepared for them a light meal of sardines, seaweed and rice. For Brittan and Page it proved to be too much and they suffered as a result during the night. Juriba calmed their anxiety to telephone the outside world, promising to take them into the capital the next morning. In the meantime, he insisted they rest and recover some of their strength. They tried to tell him that they had come down Low's Gully from the peak of Kinabalu but, since this was beyond the educated man's comprehension, they did not press the matter.

Feeling much better for having rested overnight, Brittan and Page helped Shearer into the truck to take them into the capital, Kota Kinabalu. Uppermost in the trio's minds was the fate of Mayfield and Mann. There was a universal assumption that Group B would have recognised the impossibility of their situation and withdrawn back to Kinabalu and safety. Thanking Juriba and his friends profusely, Brittan and Page went into the Travellers' Rest in anticipation of finding Mayfield and Mann. They were not there. Alarm bells started to ring. After settling Shearer they went off to seek information. Page went to the nearby Park Administration Offices close to the seafront while Brittan dashed off to the travel agents to determine whether Neill's group had already returned to Hong Kong.

Meanwhile, soon after setting off on the morning of the 6th, Mayfield and Mann had lost their trail. They began cutting through the jungle to get up onto a nearby ridge. Here they found a clearing 20 ft by 10 ft, obviously a former helicopter landing site, but it started nowhere and ended nowhere. From the top of the ridge they could see all around them, mile after mile after mile of uninterrupted jungle. To have gone on would have involved climbing back up the mountain. Mayfield decided that rather than wait for the others to catch them up, they would go down to the track to rejoin them. Once there, they shouted and screamed, but to no effect. It later transpired that Brittan's group had climbed up to the same ridge. When Brittan came back down, he found the kit which Mayfield and Mann had cast away. In Brittan's mind it was a military crime to abandon one's kit. It was then that he formulated the erroneous impression that it was he who had been abandoned.

Mayfield and Mann spent an hour and a half retracing their steps, but to no avail. The two discussed what to do next. Mayfield had the group's only compass, the other had been with Shearer and was broken in one of his falls. Taking a north-westerly bearing, Mann followed Mayfield through the jungle for two days.

In the expedition's planning stages, Mayfield and Mann had discussed what their medical box ought to contain. Mann had insisted upon a bottle of iodine. The first time it was used was on his hand. Both men had been moving through the jungle, hacking at the foliage, moving forward a foot at a time. Suddenly, Mann fell 40 ft, disappearing from sight. 'When I fell, I was so desperate not to drop the *parang*', he said. 'But it hit a root on the way down and my hand slid over the blade. It wasn't a pretty sight.' Mayfield threw a rope down to him. When he emerged, he showed Mayfield his severely lacerated hand. 'Look what I've done to my hand,' he said, raising the dripping limb for Mayfield to examine. 'Oh my God!', said Mayfield. According to Mann, it was the first time he saw real panic in Mayfield's face. Mayfield took out the bottle of iodine and said to Mann those immortal words: 'This is going to hurt you more than it's going to hurt me', whereupon he poured iodine into Mann's oozing lacerations before applying a bandage to bind the two badly cut fingers together. The bandage proved to be not very useful in the heat, humidity and wet. After four hours had elapsed, he took it off.

Mann still had his bergen with him into the second day of this phase through the jungle, a day when, as usual, he followed behind Mayfield. As darkness fell, they had come to an incline. It was not one that would normally require ropes. Its sodden surface comprised slippery earth on top of rock. As they climbed, the rain intensified and the earth gave way beneath their feet. Mayfield, losing his balance, grabbed hold of a shrub. Mann found himself marooned behind him, out in the open, trying to keep his balance, actually skating to stand still on the slippery surface. 'Move on', said Mann. 'I'm staying here', said Mayfield. It then dawned upon Mann that Mayfield had arrived at the end of his tether. Mann took off his bergen, clambered up to Mayfield, banged him on the head, gave him a piece of his mind, and took a rope from him before struggling uphill, over Mayfield, to a tree. So tired was he that he could not tie a figure of eight knot and had to make do with a 'bastard' knot. He threw the rope down to Mayfield, hitting him in the face. Mayfield climbed up the rope and collapsed beside the tree. After requesting Mayfield to tie a 'proper' knot, Mann abseiled down to his bergen, manoeuvred it onto his back and began to jumar up. When he was 20 ft up, his 'aggro' and adrenaline evaporated, taking with it his energy. His wound burst open and, because of the rain, the blood flowing from his hand gave the impression of a wound worse than it actually was. The bergen slipped from his shoulders and rolled down the hill, stopping at the very point from which it had begun.

The next morning Mayfield had recovered his composure, but both men were covered in leeches. Mayfield had one inside his upper lip. He went down to collect some items from Mann's bergen. Mann told him to pick up his wife's camera, his passport, and a bug key ring bought in the gift shop at Sabah Park. The bergen and the 'yellow peril' were left where they had landed. On reflection, Mann thought he should have told Mayfield to bring up some of his video footage, but the other items were more important to him at the time. When in hospital in England he was offered £15,000 for each video. The media wanted the story as well but, with the possibility of there being five dead bodies up on the mountain, common decency made Mann decline the offers.

Hunger was the worst aspect of this period, during which they found only three raspberries. Neither man was in real danger although the picking of opportunity food along the way confuses a body trying to adapt to hunger. They were never far from water, and although their energy levels plummeted, they could have survived for a number of weeks without food. Later that afternoon, Mann kicked something on the jungle floor. It resembled a conker and, on being opened, revealed something similar to two pomegranate seeds. They tasted good. That night, Mann was rocked by vomiting, diarrhoea and bad chest pains. He was up all night. At 5am he got into his sleeping bag, resisting all of Mayfield's entreaties for him to budge. 'Leave me here, I can't carry on, I've had it.' Mayfield then exerted himself, dragged Mann out of the sleeping bag and administered what Mann described as 'a good kick up the arse'. Half carrying Mann, Mayfield headed back towards the Gully. By virtue of standing up and walking, Mann found he could breathe, which was something he could only do with difficulty lying down. It was Tuesday 8 March and they had returned to the river, which they followed into the next day, stumbling and falling. They stayed one night in a spider- and bat-infested cave. But it was dry. They took the opportunity to get out of their wet clothing and spent the night, naked, in the one surviving sleeping bag. Their morale remained tolerably high during the day but sank at night when, more often than not, their thoughts turned to their families at home in Plymouth.

Mann's hand was extremely swollen and feeling numb. He was medically trained and suspected the limb now to be gangrenous, although it was still too soon for that:

> By then, it was in a bad state and I was convinced I would lose my fingers or even my hand. It was smelling like rotten meat and to be honest I tried to ignore it. There was nothing that could be done in the jungle. But I was only concerned that any infection could poison my body.

Mayfield led and, still using a compass, followed a bearing to the north-west. At night, they slept huddled together, soaked through, and tied together for safety. On 11 March they found an orchard of mouldy fruit. The fruit was inedible but it signified to the pair that they were approaching civilisation. On 12 March, the day after Brittan's party had reached civilisation, they emerged from the jungle near a hut where they found some dried fish wrapped in paper. Wisely, Mayfield ignored it, while Mann forced the flesh into his mouth. The sickness and diarrhoea were instantaneous. After attempting to clean up inside the hut, Mann stood outside, looking towards the direction in which they were travelling. Something above the trees caught his attention. He summoned Mayfield. 'Rich, do you see anything over there?' Not knowing what he was looking for, he sought clarification. 'What am I supposed to be looking for?' 'A television aerial,' replied Mann. 'Yes!', said Mayfield, and together they stumbled off in that direction. Then there were cattle, then some power lines drawing them on, and then there was heavenly music as though in the films, signifying the successful end of a long endeavour, and so it proved.

Mayfield had worked wonders to encourage Mann to press on. He had saved his life. But then, so had Mann bullied Mayfield when he wanted to give up. His presence had helped Mayfield who found the low, overhead jungle canopy terrifyingly claustrophobic. When at last they reached the village, Mann collapsed, the poison from his hand coursing throughout his body. A village elder allegedly hurried forward to tend to the men's more superficial injuries and called for someone to come urgently to treat Mann's hand. Mann told what happened next:

> This old lady just grabbed my hand and forced it into a large jar of what I was told was snake flesh, herbs and bones. I was too weak to argue. It felt as though my hand was on fire and when she pulled it out about 20 minutes later, the skin was spotlessly clean. It was unbelievable. The pus had gone and the open wound had been fused. My hand looked as though I'd had it in water for several hours. It was wrinkled and very clean. I just couldn't believe what had happened. The gangrene in my hand was so bad I was convinced that my fingers would be amputated at the hospital. But thanks to the jungle treatment my hand was saved.

The saga of Mann's hand was one of the major news stories to emerge from the *débâcle*. He and Mayfield, who had both suffered gravely during the course of their own odyssey, were quickly evacuated back to Hong Kong for medical treatment. Surgeons operated on the tendons in Mann's hand and sewed him up using more than 40 stitches. The staff of the British Military Hospital were intrigued by Mann's story and sought to trace the so-called medicine woman with a view to recreating the magic potion. 'Its antiseptic qualities are obviously very powerful,' said a hospital spokesman, 'and we are always keen to broaden our knowledge in these areas.' When the details of Mann's claim were received in Sabah there was more than a little scepticism. Joseph Guntavia, curator of the Sabah museum where there is a growing collection of plants used in herbal remedies, said he doubted that the cure could have been instantaneous. 'Traditional herbal preparations have been known to cure wounds, cracked and even broken bones, but it is unlikely that ailments can be cured instantly.' The story so intrigued the *Borneo Mail*'s Chief Editor, George Kanavathi, that he had it investigated in the hamlet of Melangkap Kappa where it had unfolded. The following account is based upon those investigations.

Melangkap Kappa is a predominantly Christian village of 260 people located some 60 miles from Kota Kinabalu. On Friday 11 March there had been a major religious celebration and the village chieftain, Sualin Sidon, believed it had been the sound of the bamboo instruments which may have served as the beacon to attract

Mann and Mayfield to the village. On the Saturday morning the villagers had returned to prayer, leaving the children outside to play. One of the boys, by the name of Loujin, had his attention caught by some movement on the fringe of the village. The boy took in the sight of two bony *Mat Sallehs* (whites), clad only in tattered clothing. He did not hang around, but fled into the village centre shouting that strangers were in the village and attempting to get into the house of his 60-year-old aunt, Lumpiol. One of the near-naked, bony individuals was seen trying to climb the fence into the house while another, taller and equally skinny figure was to be seen 'gulping water by the pipe stand'. This one had with him a tattered sleeping bag in which, it transpired, he kept some money, a camera and some identity documents. It was obvious from the men's demeanour that they were acutely distressed and no threat to anyone. Once this was realised, Lumpiol, whose house it was, the Chief, and a 27-year-old kindergarten teacher by the name of Roselin Marupin, went to the two men's assistance. Roselin said:

> The shorter one (Mann), was crawling and could not get over the wooden fence. He had awful cuts and wounds and was down to his underwear and shoes only. He stank and the wound on his hand was ugly. The other one (Mayfield) had already entered Lumpiol's house when I got there. He was heard to say, 'Mummy, I want to eat.' He was scrounging for food and had found some under the food cover and was grabbing at the food as though he had not eaten in days.

Neither man had eaten for seven days. Two of the women helped Mann up the stairs into Lumpiol's house. The villagers gave them water with some rice and wild boar pickles, together with some wild yam. All the while, the white men were talking, but the villagers could not comprehend. It was not long before their complaints of upset stomachs required no interpretation. Someone was despatched to go down to the village shop to buy some cereal and milk, which they 'walloped'. Attention then turned to the men's wounds, which Roselin and two of her friends bathed with hot water. A home-made potion was then applied to Mann's wound by two young women, to clean it of the dried blood and pus. 'The wound was smelly and infected, but we have experienced these sorts of wounds before and we knew it could be cured by our medicine.' Mann screamed and shouted when the medicine was administered. One of the young women described how:

> He (Mann) had his face downwards and was crying. I guess the wound hurt when we applied the lotion. We just rubbed it on after washing it with hot water and wiping it dry with a clean cloth. After the duo had a bath, we gave them some clothes belonging to Damieh's husband.

As to Mann's subsequent claims, Sualin said:

> We don't know what he is talking about. There's no witch doctor or medicine woman in this village. We did use some traditional medicine to treat his bruises, but that is about it. It is amusing to be told about an old woman thrusting his hand into a jar and after 20 minutes it became clean.

Roselin believed Mann had been hallucinating. 'He did not even look at what we were doing,' she said. 'He had his face across his right hand on the table.' Sualin said that the ointment they used was common and could be found in any chemist's shop. There were, however, some local ingredients which were added, such as the bile from a bear, and two species of centipede mixed with a type of amino acid extracted from snake fat in order to improve the lotion's potency. Apparently the lotion is used as a cure-all, but traditional medicines were becoming more and more difficult to supply due to problems of availability of some of the ingredients.

The villagers said that part of the shock at seeing these two apparitions in rags appearing among them was the fact that they were unaware of the drama going on around them. While Mann and Mayfield rested, the church service continued and the village children surrounded them in awestruck silence. Later, arrangements were made to send them down to Kota Kinabalu. The word was soon out and spread to the nearby village where Brittan's group had emerged the day before. Thus Mayfield and Mann learned that the other three were also safe. Very soon, Melangkap Kappa was invaded by rescuers looking for the other five. The two Britons offered the women who had helped them 150 Malay dollars (about £40), but they refused the gift. 'We were surprised to see them,' said Sualin:

> We had never expected anyone to walk out from the jungles on the western flank of Kinabalu. It takes a day's walking to reach just the foothills of the mountain, and if they say they were lost for over a week, they must have had a tough time. It is rather dangerous if one does not know the way. Even our own people seldom venture out that far.

Thus, within the space of 24 hours and along different paths, the two groups of whippets, the able and physically fit, had reached safety, but *en route* had come so close to death. Back up the mountain there were still, of course, the two leaders and the three Chinese novices. They had passed their point of no return and, in view of the difficulties which had beset the whippets, the prospects for the oldies and novices must be rated as extremely bleak. They took the whole of 1 March to execute the six abseils down to the floor of the Gully. Here they found Group A's camp site and settled down for the night. They were up early the next morning to recover the ropes used to get them into the Gully before proceeding downstream. The rain fell heavily that afternoon, making their progress over the rocks exceptionally difficult. So bad did the conditions become that they stopped the day's trek early and spent the night in caves.

The next morning Neill checked the ration state and found that they had but two days' remaining. He emphasised to the group the serious predicament they were facing and stressed that the two days' supply would have to stretch to six. On the evening of 3 March they took shelter in Battleship Cave, recommencing their journey at 8am on 4 March. The 4th was a significant date for it was the day by which the group should have returned to Park Headquarters to indicate both that they were safe and that their expedition had been concluded. In reality, they had a further three weeks to suffer before being rescued. They made slow progress through rattan, vines and pitcher plants. Foster had injured his leg and chest, and each of the Chinese soldiers was suffering from one kind of injury or another. Neill discussed the situation with Foster. Neither man could conceal his concern from the other, but neither indicated that he felt the situation to be critical.

On 5 March, Neill and his group pushed on over rocks which had once been dry and safe stepping stones, but which had now become slippery and dangerous from the rain which had resumed that morning. Where, they wondered, were New's Pools? It wasn't as though it was possible to have missed them. Eventually, just off a slight bend they saw the pools, instantly recognisable from the slides that New had shown them. It had taken Group B ten days to reach this point, eight days longer than it had taken the underrated New and Pinfield. The two officers knew from their research that it was from this point that matters would become seriously difficult. But suddenly, being there and facing the reality of the chasm in front of them, the message was most emphatically driven home. They could see so clearly now why the civilians had not gone on but had instead broken out to the right. Cheung, who had been scouting around, found a new, blue sling under the rising water. This confirmed that Group A had passed this way, but the discovery of a rope lower down and off to the right seemed to suggest that Mayfield had contrived to avoid the water.

Obviously the water level was now higher than when Group A had been there. What Neill desperately needed was the advice of his expert rock climber. He did not have the confidence or desire to risk the group by negotiating the waterfalls. The developing buoyant flair and panache of the Chinese quite suddenly evaporated. They did not like or relish what they saw in front of them. Neither did Foster. They decided to break out to the right as New and Pinfield had done, but for them it was not dry under foot as it had been for their predecessors. They could not get purchase on the muddy incline, falling back as soon as they had gone forward. As each minute passed, so the mountain taxed their energy and, by the approach of dusk, they were exhausted and had made little forward progress. Neill ordered his men to withdraw back beyond the point from which they had surveyed the pools. Cheung was in the lead, fighting his way through the undergrowth above the roaring stream. As a last resort, Neill told Cheung to abseil down to the river to see whether there was any shelter there before the light was completely gone. Down went the Hong Kong Chinese man. By luck, Cheung came upon a cave with room to accommodate the whole group. They named it after him, Kevin's Cave. It was to become their involuntary home for the next three weeks.

The group woke on 6 March to the continuing foul weather outside and stayed put in their sleeping bags until late. Getting up out of their sodden sleeping bags in their sodden clothes was not the highlight of the day. Outside in the Gully the water level continued to rise. They occupied themselves by putting out an SOS sign and a figure 5 (implying there were five people), marked by large boulders. This act, more than any other, reflected their implicit acceptance of the fact that they were now in serious difficulties. The ground was reasonably open there; not so open as to permit a helicopter to land, but certainly sufficiently open for a helicopter to winch them out. In addition, they set out a reflective blanket and coloured clothing in the hope of attracting the attention of the helicopter which they felt certain would soon be looking for them. This was a fond hope because, for various reasons, the fact that they were missing would not be actioned until 15 March.

'The east is east and the west is west and ne'er the twain shall meet,' goes the saying. In common with all such sayings, this one contains variable elements of truth. In this case, it is most important that a distinction is made regarding the relationship which developed between the British and Chinese soldiers on Neill's exercise, and the norm which existed between the British and Chinese members of formed units in Hong Kong. There is an understandable difference in attitude and training standards between locally employed soldiers engaged in monotonous, routine, general duties in a Supply Depot as opposed to the standards of Chinese soldiers who have served with distinguished professionalism in general transport, pack transport and maritime units. For example, 29 Transport Squadron had a world class motorcycle display team. Without exception, in all the Hong Kong units and detachments, the leadership was well acquainted with east–west cultural differences and also had a good knowledge of each individual and his capabilities. Neither Neill nor Foster knew Cheung, Chow or Lam, two of whom, through no fault of their own, were entirely unsuitable for participation in the exercise. When later questioned on this point, Neill, somewhat disingenuously said, 'I did not choose them'. Moreover, the British soldiers on the exercise, who met the Chinese lads for the first time on the plane to Brunei, had an expectation of their level of training which they did not have and, indeed, had no cause to achieve. The inbound British soldiers had no reason to know any better and, consequently, made a quite serious misassumption. In that respect, there was a clear breakdown in communications.

There was little empathy or camaraderie between the British officers and their Chinese subordinates. Even solutions to their problem were rigorously distinct. The Chinese chose to eat little and undertake the minimum of activity, thereby saving energy. The officers preferred to be active for some of the time, to take their minds off their predicament. Consequently it was they who were doing most of the chores around the camp site: something which deep down, albeit irrationally, annoyed Foster. At other times, the Chinese sat and watched the officers playing chess and Scrabble on Neill's pocket set. There were times when Foster sat down to write up his diary of events. On the cover he had written: 'All notes in this book are the copyright of R.E. Foster, and on his death, of his wife, Mrs J. Foster, of the above address.' The irony of the *débâcle* of Exercise Gulley Heights, for which both officers were by no means blameless, was that if it had passed without incident in the same way as 99 per cent of the British Army's adventurous training exercises, it would have attracted absolutely no attention whatsoever.

The decision to stay put to conserve energy had been the right one. To Neill and Foster it seemed only a matter of time before rescuers would find them. The warning should by now have been sounded at Park Headquarters; they had left kit with both New and Powell, and it would not be long before Hong Kong sparked. The rejection of Powell's offer to raise the alarm if they had not returned proved to be an error of judgement. It was one less arrow in the quiver. That the reconnaissance party had got through to raise the alarm was even a remote chance. However, if they were dead, thought Neill, to what degree had they brought it upon themselves by separating? As events would show, that separation probably saved all their lives.

On 8 March, Neill and Foster decided to reconnoitre possible escape routes to take the next day. Neill took the west ridge, Foster the east ridge. The fact that Mayfield had taken the only two *parangs* they possessed, contributed to a build-up of tension and depression. Logically, it had made sense for Mayfield to take the machetes, for the intention had been to clear the path for Group B following on behind. Neill discovered the advance group's tracks and their camp site up on the west ridge. He also found a small amount of food, which raised his morale. However, the reconnaissance revealed that an attempted escape would be a high risk endeavour. In Neill's mind, he knew sitting tight and awaiting rescue was the best course. But all the time, he must have been aware, at the end of all this, how much better it would be presentationally for the group to have saved themselves rather than put the authorities to all the effort that a rescue would involve. However, it proved to be mightily difficult to just sit there and wait. Wait for what?

Foster's morale was at rock bottom. It was raining, he stumbled in and out of the water, slipped on rocks, and found his way barred by rattan which he had no means of cutting. When he returned, having failed in his mission, Foster let off steam by venting his anger in his diary upon the Chinese. They had said at the outset that this mission was not for them, and they had been right. They had been poorly briefed and poorly prepared. The fault was not theirs. However, Foster wrote of them:

> They had decided not to play, 'too weak' being the stock reply. Robert (Neill) and I have been carrying them like passengers almost from Day One. A tremendous liability. Acting almost like children, having to be told/asked to do everything – and even then with little enthusiasm.

Obviously fed up and depressed, such comments, even if true, help to let off steam and, as long as they remain between the diary's covers, no harm is done. Unfortunately this was not to be the case for, even having had time for quiet reflection after being rescued, Foster allowed these comments to be published in the London *Daily Mail* on 4 April 1994 (see page 125). Foster clearly had no sensitivity towards his subordinates.

The inactivity was now playing on the minds of Neill and Foster. Just as the advance party had used New's and Pinfield's progress down the Gully, so too did the British officers. They had plenty of time to talk on their own, and the focus of their attention was invariably the best way of breaking out. If New and Pinfield could break out from New's Pools, they reasoned that so could they. There was no plan to take the Chinese with them. Foster asserted that they were too weak to go, and they agreed to remain behind as a rear party. According to Cheung, however, after discussions with Lam and Chow they asked to accompany Neill and Foster, but their entreaties were rejected by Neill. 'I should have been allowed to take part in the rescue attempt,' said Cheung, 'because I was the fittest in the group'.

The officers set off at 8.45am on 11 March with slimmed-down bergens, but they had been severely weakened by their ordeal and made little progress that day. It had taken Mann and Mayfield a further ten days to move from this point until they emerged, more dead than alive, out of the jungle. Neill and Foster did not have the skill, strength or expertise of Mann and Mayfield. They had absolutely no idea what lay ahead of them, other than an instinctive desire to do something. Leaving the Chinese as they did, however, was a further breach of all the rules. Neill's expedition had now fragmented into four parts. Questions soon to appear in the press regarding his command and control are therefore unsurprising. As part of their preparations, they collected all the available cash. In total, there was over £900 to be used to finance a rescue. Neill left the three Chinese men with one hundred Malaysian Dollars saying, jokingly, that it was for a 'mountain burger'. Sometimes the British humour went over the Chinese heads.

Neill and Foster spent 12 March climbing steep, slippery inclines, grabbing plants for purchase as their feet continually gave way on the muddy topsoil. They soon realised that the grain of the land was taking them away from where they wanted to go. Still, on Sunday the 13th their hopes were raised by the sound of a helicopter. On two occasions Foster saw a white helicopter. (It was at this time that Eric Wong and Brittan were in the air, checking the exits from the Gully into the Panataran, having wrongly assumed that Group B would have made better progress than they had.)

Neill and Foster rationed their food to a bare minimum, half a packet of soup and a biscuit a day being a not unusual diet. Eventually they had to face the fact that they were achieving nothing of value by proceeding, and duly decided to return to Kevin's Cave. For some reason, they stopped short of the cave on the night of 13 March, presumably on the assumption that their appearance earlier than planned would not benefit the Chinese soldiers' morale. But Cheung, Lam and Chow had no reason to believe with confidence that the officers would in due course return with a helicopter to rescue them. Rather than sit around in Kevin's Cave, they had jointly decided that on 14 March they would follow the path taken by the British officers. Both groups were therefore mightily surprised to meet one another just further up the valley. Neill had been talking into Foster's camera when they became aware of crashing in the undergrowth coming their way. Neill showed his annoyance at meeting the Chinese, while Foster was dismissive of what he saw as their foolhardy gesture:

> They had no food, would not have the energy and would find it impossible to do what Robert (Neill) and I had done. They had thought they could follow us to safety. Luckily we were there to stop them.

Back in Kevin's Cave, morale sank. Thoughts turned to loved ones at home who might never be seen again. Each man could see in the others' faces the gaunt, harrowed look which was worn by himself. Of one thing, thankfully, they were not short, and that was water – one of the sources of their misfortune. The tone of Foster's diary continued in a distinctly 'them and us' manner, the Chinese soldiers and he and 'Robert'. He wrote about food, estimating that he and Neill had at least seven days' worth of meagre rations remaining, but observed that the 'HK (Hong Kong) lads' had almost finished theirs. 'What will they want', he wrote, '... us to *share* with them?' He wrote of how the officers had tried to impress upon the Chinese from the outset the need to keep and conserve rations, '... and until we went into Easy Valley they had been ditching theirs ... we made them buy noodles, chocolate, tinned fish and biscuits before we set off'. Yet again Foster had the insensitivity to allow his unsubstantiated criticisms to appear in the national press. Cheung observed how, of the two officers, Foster was the least forthcoming.

In fact, Foster's assumption and allegation was misconstrued. The Chinese soldiers had pooled their food and established a reserve store in the event that their sojourn on the rocks around Kevin's Cave became more protracted than they dared think. The claim that they had ditched rations was to repeat the untrue allegation of a barrack room lawyer within the group. A man who, during the course of the Inquiry, Brittan had found necessary 'to brief up'.

Ears remained pricked and eyes scanned a sky which more often than not was hidden by cloud and mist. Why, they wondered, could they not see search aircraft? Foster was worried about his wife's anxieties, yet it was not until now, 15 March, that a priority signal was sent from Hong Kong to the United Kingdom advising that five Service personnel on Exercise Gulley Heights were overdue. The five's torment still had many days to run. Their destiny had slipped from theirs to other people's hands. Foster became worried by nightmares, Chow believed he would not get out alive, and still it rained. It was probably the rain that on 16 March loosened the rocks which came hurtling down into the group's camp. They scattered and, once all was quiet, they surveyed the scene. Chow, whose instincts had told him he would not survive, was found buried under three boulders. After being set free, his injuries seemed minor in relation to what they might have been. His back was hurt and later in the day he started hallucinating. It rained all day on 17 March and the group remained in their sleeping bags until a torrent of water swept through their sleeping area, forcing them to move. We shall leave the group at Kevin's Cave to persevere with the routine which was now becoming the feature of each day, and turn to the details of their rescue.

5
The Rescue

Mann and Mayfield were given a lift from the village to the Travellers' Rest in Kota Kinabalu. After the two had met Brittan, and after both sides had said, 'What the hell happened to you?', Mann asked, 'Where's the Colonel?'. Brittan explained how he had searched but could find no trace of the other five. 'I have arranged with the Head Warden (Eric Wong) to go up on a helicopter reconnaissance tomorrow (Sunday),' he said. Both Mann and Mayfield were in desperate straits, emaciated, and their bodies ripped by rocks and branches. They arrived dressed in clothing given to them by the villagers. Mayfield suffered body cramps and Mann's most pressing infliction was diarrhoea. Drained of energy, Mann went outside and sat on the verandah of his room in a half trance. The next thing he became aware of was being examined by an English woman. He believed Miss X to have been a vet on holiday. He did not know her name. Her being a vet seemed strangely appropriate to him. She looked him over, looked at his hand, turned to Brittan and said, 'We've got to get this man to hospital immediately.' Off they went in a car and Mann and Shearer were duly admitted to the city hospital. The English woman was quite clearly aghast at the state in which she found the five soldiers, three of whom needed to be hospitalised for various periods. What disturbed her most, however, was the account of another five being lost up on the mountain. If they were in anything like the condition of the five she had met, she reasoned, their lives were seriously threatened.

On the evening of Saturday 12 March, Mike Scott, the Honorary British Representative in Sabah and Manager of the Hong Kong and Shanghai Bank, was at home in Kota Kinabalu celebrating his wife's birthday. The telephone rang. It was a young woman insisting that she should talk to him urgently. He listened to her account of how she had met some British soldiers in The Travellers' Rest. She told him how ill they were, and how she had taken them to Queen Elizabeth Hospital where Mann and Shearer had been admitted. What was worse, she said, was that there were other members of their team lost on the mountain and no one was doing anything about their rescue. Scott thanked her profusely for her information. Although a resident of Kota Kinabalu, he did not know of a Travellers' Rest, but did know a Travellers' Lodge, which he rang. No, they had no British soldiers booked in there. Scott bundled his wife into their car and went into the city to find the Travellers' Rest, but to no avail. It is a typical back-packer's hostel on the fourth floor of a shabby building close to the Parks Administrative Building and not the type of residence used by the average holidaymaker.

On Sunday he rang Sabah Outward Bound and asked the manager whether he knew anything of three British soldiers in hospital. The manager confirmed that he knew of the expedition but did not know when they were due to return. He suggested that Scott should ring Robert New. 'When that call came through, I felt an immediate sense of guilt,' said New.

> Foster had even left his computer with me for safekeeping but, with a hectic business life, I had not noticed their failure to return. I did, however, know where the Travellers' Rest was and, together with Mike Scott, we went there without delay.

At the hostel, the two civilians met four of the soldiers. 'They were there waiting for the others (Group B) to come out,' said Scott,

> I rang the High Commission in Kuala Lumpur. They knew of the expedition but were unaware that there was a problem. We were not entirely convinced there was a problem, due to Corporal Brittan's insistence that Colonel Neill and his group had almost certainly gone back up the Gully.

'We did not want to start alarming people,' explained Brittan,

> We knew we had to check before we blew the whistle, fully aware that time was against us. We thought we could sort it out in-house. We checked the hotels, Sabah Parks and the airlines, without luck. Then Mayfield and Mann appeared. They were in a bad state and they and Shearer were taken to hospital where Shearer and Mann were admitted. Mann had his hand treated and Shearer had his legs drained

> of fluid. Although Mayfield was not admitted, he suffered stomach cramps. It was obvious to me that they should be evacuated back to Hong Kong.

Thus the decision to ring the big alarm bells was taken off Brittan's shoulders by the Honorary British Representative. Scott then set about trying to discover what he could concerning the progress of the aims and execution of Neill's expedition.

The medical staff treating Mann were kindness itself, but after what he had been through he found the relative isolation difficult to bear. No one at that time had linked his particular situation with the larger problem. He lay on the bed, being administered with liquid to remedy his dehydration. His requests for food were politely denied. On Sunday 13 March, clad only in his shorts, he discharged himself from hospital. Outside, he took a taxi from the rank and said 'Kentucky Fried Chicken'. He could not remember his hostel's name or location, but did remember that it was close to the designated fast food outlet. When the taxi drew up outside the hotel, he asked the driver to go upstairs to the fourth floor and bring help. He had no money, but also his recurring diarrhoea had left him in a mess. Brittan and Mayfield hurried down, paid off the unhappy driver and helped Mann upstairs. Mann was well aware that he needed medical treatment but, without offence to the Malaysian hospital, he knew that he personally would be more at ease in a British hospital and, at that time, he had in mind the British Military Hospital in Hong Kong.

'Brittan was everywhere, quietly, efficiently, getting things organised. He was doing a lot,' said Mann, whose thoughts turned to his home, to his wife and son. Extraordinary as it may seem, he remembered that Sunday 13 March was Mothers' Day. His wife received the oddest of telephone calls. He said to her:

> If the Ministry of Defence tell you I am missing, I am alive. Don't tell anyone things have gone wrong, but five of the group are lost on the mountain. If the press contact you, don't talk.

That night, as he sat alone out on the verandah, watching the orangey-red sky darken, he reflected upon the recent past. He saw the haunted, worried faces of the inexperienced Chinese and heard their repeated pleas to him, 'Bob, Bob, we don't want to go.' He cursed himself. 'I should have been stronger,' he said to himself over and over again and, as he sat there, he wept for Cheung, Lam and Chow.

As a result of a visit by Page to the Park Administration Building, Eric Wong, the Head Warden, was duly called in. He remembered the Lieutenant Colonel and the Major passing through and had seen their comprehensive array of kit. They had impressed upon him how well qualified they were and how the Gully was well within their capabilities. 'I wasn't going to teach a duck to swim,' said Wong,

> They were trained people from the famous British army. I did not check their rations, they are Europeans, we are Asians. Our food is heavier. There was, however, within their can-do philosophy a hint of over-optimism. I told them that they wouldn't appear as soon as 4 March. From my own experience I recognised that their time and space appreciation was flawed. I therefore added on some extra days. Obviously I did not want to raise a false alarm. Delays on and around the mountain are quite normal.

Wong had begun his check for Neill's group in the neighbouring villages on 11 March. On that day, Brittan's group had emerged suspecting some of their colleagues to be in trouble. The next day, Wong sent in the Rangers. When Mann and Mayfield appeared on 12 March, Wong fully expected Neill's group to be following behind. Brittan was not so certain. Wong therefore hired a Bell Huey reconnaissance helicopter for Sunday 13 March. He made rendezvous with Brittan at the airfield and together they went up to search through the exits out of the Gully. The wind and cloud that day restricted their search to the lower part of the Gully. Even on the clearest of days a helicopter would not normally venture into the Gully because of the danger. A number of helicopters had been lost on Mount Kinabalu. Back at the airfield, Wong and Brittan discussed who was to raise the alarm. Brittan volunteered for the time being and Wong returned to the mountain to organise more men to search the villages and jungle terrain below 4,000 feet.

On the morning of Tuesday 15 March, Mann said to Mayfield, 'I have to get into hospital. Go and book our flights to Hong Kong.' Without argument, Mayfield went off and, using his Barclaycard, paid the £206 each for a seat on Wednesday's flight to Hong Kong. On the Tuesday, Mann took a call from a Lieutenant Commander Williams, the British Naval Attaché in Kuala Lumpur. He enquired after Mann and the others. Mann told him what he knew and offered the information that the next day, he and Mayfield were departing for Hong Kong for medical attention. The naval officer then said, 'I shall be in Kota Kinabalu tomorrow. You must stay where you are so that I can debrief you.' That order pole-axed a sergeant extremely concerned about his health and with a hand the likes of which would have graced a Hammer Horror film. Shocked, he put down the receiver. Fifteen minutes later the telephone rang again. It was the Naval Attaché in a contrite mood. 'You're there, I'm not, and you're in a better position to know of your needs than I. I shall tell the authorities in Hong Kong of your intentions.' Shortly afterwards, Shearer came into Mann's room and said, 'There's a general on the phone, wants to talk to you.' Not for a moment was Mann taken in by this cynical press ploy. A soldier knew instinctively that generals were not accustomed to ringing up sergeants in their hostel rooms. He took the call. The man wanted precise and detailed information of Neill's group's situation. 'How many battalions were required?', he asked. Mann deliberately talked gibberish and, satisfied that he had left the caller none the wiser, replaced the receiver. He then forgot all about the incident until something said at the Board of Inquiry concentrated his mind, bringing a flush to his cheeks. 'Who', said the Chairman of the Board, 'took Brigadier General Hussin's telephone call asking for the information that he, as Director of Combined Search and Rescue Operations, urgently required?'

The fact that Neill and his group really were missing somewhere on Mount Kinabalu was a conclusion drawn at roughly the same time by different people in different parts of the world fed from different sources. Attendant upon that conviction there ensued concurrent interconnected activity in the United Kingdom, Kuala Lumpur, Kota Kinabalu and Hong Kong. Brittan contacted the Supply people in Hong Kong on 14 March. Wong had given him the name left by Neill as the point of contact – Major Ramsden.

'Please put me in touch with Major Ramsden,' said Brittan.

'Major Ramsden is on leave,' came the reply.

'It is imperative that you put me in contact,' insisted Brittan.

'We cannot,' said the voice in Hong Kong. 'Major Ramsden is on leave outside the Territory; he is in Borneo.'

An exasperated Brittan left a message, the gist of which told of the other five's predicament. The Supply representatives in turn got in touch with Headquarters British Forces Hong Kong. It was a Chinese holiday and the message was left in the hands of a clerk.

Not until the 15th did someone in Supply react to the serious message which had come out of Kota Kinabalu. A priority signal was sent, informing the UK that the five Service personnel were overdue. Meanwhile, in Kuala Lumpur, the diplomatic channels had checked out Mike Scott's information and, at midday Hong Kong time, HQ British Forces were informed by the Defence Adviser, Kuala Lumpur, that five soldiers were missing. Hong Kong immediately informed the Ministry of Defence, Whitehall. The Assistant Chief of the Defence Staff (Operations) accordingly delegated national command to the Commander British Forces Hong Kong, Major General John Foley, who was to co-ordinate British input from Hong Kong. At about the same time, the Ministry of Defence contacted the Warrant Officer, Mountain Rescue Services UK, to assemble a team of mountain rescue experts and their equipment to leave that day, Tuesday the 15th, for a search and rescue operation in Borneo.

Never before in the 51-year history of the Mountain Rescue Service had an overseas mountain rescue operation been launched from the United Kingdom. There had been no prior requirement. It was a day of instant decisions. The warning order arrived at 9.45am with the executive order to go at 1.45pm. They had to be at Heathrow at 10pm to catch their plane, Malaysian Airways Flight 001 for Kuala Lumpur. The search co-ordinator, Warrant Officer Alastair Haveron, set about the team selection, fully aware that he had to maintain cover out on the ground at home. There are six Mountain Rescue Teams located at strategic positions throughout the United Kingdom. One decision influencing selection was a preference for men who had recent experience of working at altitude. Four men were called up from the Mountain Rescue teams at RAF Kinloss and RAF Leuchars, both in Scotland, while two each were taken from RAF Leeming in North Yorkshire, RAF Stafford in mid-England, RAF Valley in Wales, and RAF St Athan in Cornwall.

Haveron had little to go on but, in a short period of time, a flow of excellent information became available from the Royal Geographic Society's Expedition Advisory Centre. There was also the concurrent movement problem of gathering together the men and their equipment. As to what equipment to take, Haveron played it off the cuff with emphasis on taking standard yet lightweight equipment. They took, for example, lightweight, roll-up stretchers, and had the good fortune to be able to borrow the standard Bell stretcher from the Sabah Outward Bound School. The plan was that, other than the St Athan men, the mountain rescue team would assemble at RAF Brize Norton in Oxfordshire. The teams from Scotland and Leeming flew down in a maritime reconnaissance Nimrod aircraft of 120 Squadron RAF, the two from Wales arrived in a search and rescue helicopter, while those from Stafford reached Brize Norton by road. When complete, that part of the team and their equipment left Brize Norton by bus for Heathrow. Once there, they were joined by the two men from St Athan, an army doctor from Aldershot, and two combat survival instructors. Haveron had with him a ticket for 2,500 lb (1,135 kg) of excess baggage. Malaysia Airlines would not accept it, passing the whole paraphernalia through, gratis, as personal baggage.

The previous day, Monday 14th, Major Tony Schumacher had departed from Heathrow on a British Airways flight for Hong Kong, *en route* for Brunei where he was the officer commanding the Training Team located at the British Army Jungle Warfare School. His plane touched down at Hong Kong's Kai Tak airport on Tuesday 15 March (Hong Kong and Kota Kinabalu are both eight hours ahead of GMT). The plan was that he should stay in the Territory that night prior to taking up a charter seat to Brunei on Wednesday 16th. He found a note pushed under the door of his room. It told him of a problem in Sabah and said that his name was among a number being considered to go to Kota Kinabalu to become Commander British Rescue Operations. The note concluded with instructions for him to report to Headquarters British Forces Hong Kong the next day for briefing. This was one hot potato not of their making which Hong Kong could have done without.

At 2pm on Tuesday 15 March, the second Hari Raya (that is the second day of the most important of the Islamic religious festivals and to the Muslim what Christmas is to the Christian), Major Rahin, Operations Major of Malaysia's 5th Infantry Brigade, took receipt of urgent operational orders. The orders had come from the Ministry of Defence in Kuala Lumpur through Headquarters of the 1st Division, located in Kuching. The Commander of 5th Infantry Brigade, Sandhurst-trained Brigadier General Hussin Bin Yussof, was nominated to be the Director of Combined Search and Rescue Operations and was to use his own sub-units to find the five missing British army soldiers.

The Brigadier and all his officers were off duty and, for the most part, were dressed in the customary *sarong* as they each, independently celebrated the holiday. Brigadier Hussin was at home when he received his orders. He immediately summoned to his house those officers who would be required to implement his plan. Concurrent action was brought into play in order to have the first company (they were later reinforced by two more) ready to deploy into the jungle at 2am on 16 March so as to be in a position to begin the search at first light.

The Brigadier's officers and men were conscious that they were involved in something very serious and were under no illusions as to the difficulty of their mission. 'Everything comes back to the mission,' explained the Brigadier. 'Mine was to search for, locate and rescue the five missing British military personnel in Low's Gully.' No one in 5th Brigade underrated the area; an area known for its steep, very rocky and difficult terrain. Whereas technical expertise could ensure the establishment of satisfactory communications between the Operations Centre in the brigade's Lok Kawi Camp, 10 miles (16 km) to the south of Kota Kinabalu, the companies in the field, Park HQ, the Brigadier's house (where communications were manned for 24 hours) and the Hyatt Hotel, no one could help the infantry with the unenviable, physical task of searching such unforgiving and inhospitable terrain. The life of boots could be counted in days, but the Malaysian soldiers persevered with their search without complaint.

Duly given the job to co-ordinate British military activity and interests in Sabah, the now Local Lieutenant Colonel Schumacher arrived at Kota Kinabalu's international airport at 6.55pm on Wednesday 16 March. Later that evening he met two members of Brunei Garrison who had been sent to assist him: the adjutant of 6 Gurkha Rifles and a Warrant Officer of the Royal Logistic Corps with experience of adventurous training activities. Shortly after, a liaison officer from Lok Kawi Camp introduced himself, saying that his brigade commander had instructed him to afford them all necessary assistance. At 10pm, Schumacher was back at the airport to meet Warrant Officer Haveron and the mountain rescue group. They had changed to a Boeing 737 at Kuala Lumpur and, after travelling for 26 hours, had now reached their final destination. Malaysian military transport took them all to the Hyatt Hotel in the city centre for a briefing based on the best available information. Schumacher chaired the briefing which went on until 3am on the 17th, helped by Brittan who was assisted by Page in giving an eye witness account of what the RAF men should expect up on the mountain. Schumacher was frank: 'We have no precise idea where they are or the route they took.' Those simple facts had their unwelcome impact upon the first few days of the rescue attempt.

The arrival of a public relations officer, Arthur Murray from Joint Services' Public Relations, Hong Kong, signified a consciousness of the interest the rescue operation would generate for the world press. In a matter of hours, press representatives from Reuters, AFP, the *Sunday Times, Daily Mirror, South China Morning Post* and Star TV had booked into the Hyatt Hotel. Also to arrive early on Wednesday 16 March was Lieutenant Commander Cliff Williams, Royal Navy, from the military staff of the British High Commission in Kuala Lumpur. 'He', explained Schumacher,

> was the link with the political side and the man with the gold card. He told me that as far as our people in Kuala Lumpur were concerned, this was a Malaysian-led operation. My role was to assist and provide expertise where the Malaysians required assistance, for example in mountain rescue.

The Consular Representative, Mike Scott, helped in making introductions and giving advice.

At first light on 17 March, Schumacher was up and about to take half the RAF mountain rescue men down to the airfield. Expressed in simple terms, the division of responsibility for the search operation between the Malaysians and British had the Malaysians – soldiers, rangers and police – searching along the Panataran River and up into the Gully, while the RAF mountain rescue men attacked the Gully from the top. Based on the information he had received that night, Warrant Officer Haveron divided his group into two equal teams led by Flight Sergeant Smith from Kinloss and Sergeant Carroll from St Athan. The plan was to fly Group 1 at 6.30am from the airfield and insert them on the north side of the mountain at around 8,500 feet, while Group 2 arranged the equipment and prepared to go by road once it was ready. The Royal Malaysian Airforce Sikorsky Nuri took off with Group 1, as planned, but the cloud and topography conspired to force them to land well below Park Headquarters, close to a local medical centre. The accompanying Malaysian officers commandeered two willing teachers and their cars and, in that manner, Group 1 arrived at the roadhead in the National Park. Here they met Eric Wong and, after a ground orientation they set out at 5pm, arriving at the planned advanced operating base at Panar

Laban at 9pm. The weather was dreadful, with low cloud and heavy rain. Eric Wong had made available two porters to help with the ferrying of rescue equipment up the mountain to Panar Laban and on to the Easy Valley col. Meanwhile Haveron led Group 2 by road up to Park HQ. The building there is excellent – a great deal of space, a custom-made cinema for briefings, good restaurant facilities and really good local cooks. Haveron, the medical officer, the combat survival instructors and a civilian rescue expert made their contribution to an operations cell up on the mountain.

Communication was always seen to be the problem to beat but that problem was solved by the introduction of a multiplicity of means including land line, cellular telephones and marine band UHF radios. Very rapidly, what was happening on the mountain could be speedily transmitted to the operations centre at Lok Kawi Camp and to the information centre at the Hyatt Hotel. The British administrative cell at the Hyatt produced a daily situation report which was sent to Hong Kong for release with any additional comments that Headquarters British Forces Hong Kong thought should be added. Although there was quite significant media representation in Kota Kinabalu, Hong Kong is a substantial regional communications and information hub, so much so that most of the information regarding developments on the mountain were drawn off in Hong Kong rather than Sabah. This caused some difficulty for staff officers who were unable to answer the media's *ad hoc* questions because they did not have the right answers. The understandable desire to remain optimistic did result in some misleading information being disseminated. On 17 March, for example, the Hong Kong press were told that when Neill's group was last seen they had been on half rations, which was translated as 1,500 calories a day. The spokesman also said the men would be able to supplement their rations with fruit and edible protein, including earthworms, snakes and insects.

Roger Goodwin, the MOD Director of Public Relations in Hong Kong found that, other than wars such as the Falklands and the Gulf, the Gulley Heights saga was 'without question quite the most intensive and sustained period of media pressure on a single subject that I have known in nearly 30 years of MOD press relations'. So intensive was the media-feeding frenzy that it is now used as a public relations case study for instructional purposes. For some three weeks, weekends included, the Hong Kong team spent 12–15 hour days dealing with nothing but the Kinabalu story; mornings updating the

Hong Kong and Asia media, afternoons and evenings the same thing with the British press. Meanwhile, in Kota Kinabalu, Roger Goodwin's civilian deputy, Arthur Murray, found himself for days at a time imprisoned in his hotel room by the sheer volume of incoming media calls. During one period of several days, he was unable to finish a single meal, even though served in his room. During the final two days, when Neill's group was discovered and rescued, he logged no less than 165 separate, live, radio and television interviews with international broadcasting organisations. In addition, he had to deal with large numbers of in-country international journalists.

The RAF's Group 1 was up early on 18 March to face another day of poor weather. By 7am they had reached the Easy Valley col where they established a solo radio link before commencing their search and descent into the top part of the Gully. At Lone Tree they established an equipment cache and descended the first two abseil pitches before running out of time and rope. Behind them, Group 2 moved up to the advance base. Down below, at the foot of the Gully, an Alouette helicopter with two RAF men acting as observers conducted a reconnaissance. What made the task of these various agencies infinitely more complicated was not just Neill's decision not to take radios but that he had also failed to take with him smoke flares or directional search and rescue beacons. The visual signals are deemed to be hazardous cargo on aircraft and obviously could not have accompanied the team to Brunei. However, it would have been possible to secure the same in either Brunei or Sabah. It must be assumed that the failure to take directional beacons was due to an oversight. On the 18th, the two officers at Kevin's Cave constantly debated among themselves the reasons why the whippets had slipped their leash and what the hope for rescue could be. The officers had done all they could do in improvising with the available resources to attract attention.

On 19 March the RAF's Group 2 took more rope down into the Gully, thus enabling an overall improvement in the depth of the descent by 1,000ft. The weather was bad again. Flash waterfalls and impassable rock pools forced them to postpone the search. The supply of rope had been exhausted and it was dark. What the rescuers did find was an abseiling rope still fixed to a rock face and the remains of some powdered food rations. Group 2 camped out at Lone Tree. The next day they returned to Panar Laban close to exhaustion, having been kept awake all night by the continuous rain.

Haveron had a meeting to discuss the way forward. During the course of the discussion the experts decided that it was virtually impossible to progress further until the rain stopped. The rain had also served to make the sloping slabs wet and treacherous. It was no longer safe to have 16 men carrying heavy loads traversing such dangerous terrain without the use of safety ropes. This rescue attempt was not going to be plain sailing.

'When the RAF teams began their search into the Gully,' explained Schumacher,

> they attempted to achieve a day's worth of activity and then withdraw back to Panar Laban. There were occasions when they spent a number of nights out on the mountain but generally, the RAF operated a daily cycle. This system caused some comment to be raised by observers at the scene but it is important to remember the *modus operandi* of the RAF Mountain Rescue Teams.

Theirs is essentially a low level mountain rescue function to a height of up to 3,000 ft, having first been choppered in close to the rescue site. They work in short bursts, do the job, then withdraw. 'On Kinabalu,' continued Schumacher,

> it was not that they did not have among their number some with experience of working at high altitude, but that collectively they had no experience of that type of terrain or the use of the type of support available to them. The perception began to emerge that they had to reassess their *modus operandi* in the light of the nature of the prevailing unfavourable conditions.

The public just could not imagine the nature and severity of the terrain over which the mountain rescue men were working. Admittedly access was very close to the tourist track, but so too is Commando Cauldron, said to be the biggest free abseil drop in the world and so named after the Commandos who failed to conquer it. 'What was being asked of the men,' said Schumacher, 'was to go down into totally uncharted territory, working at altitude and with little rest between forays. A number of those men made efforts of superhuman endeavour.' For men used to policing the highlands of Scotland, for example, the problems to be faced on Kinabalu were of a different degree of magnitude. RAF Kinloss's Flight Sergeant Jim Smith described the place as 'both awe inspiring and very foreboding. It is shut in from all sides. The walls lurch straight up for hundreds of feet, blocking out the sun.'

The British planners in the Hyatt were working in support of Brigadier Hussin's staff on a daily basis to try to ensure that there was a pattern to the search. Activity began to shift to the Operations Centre at Lok Kawi Camp. The first press conference was held at the Hyatt but subsequent ones were held at the camp. The military authorities recognised that the press had a general need for information so, after their daily co-ordination meeting, a formal press briefing would follow. The principal difficulty facing the planners was the uncertainty as to whether Neill had descended into the Gully beyond the point of no return. According to the Parks team, who had spoken to Neill the morning he had come to their office to seek permission to embark upon the expedition, he had said that if what he wanted to do proved impossible, he would go off and climb elsewhere in the Park. The would-be rescuers were therefore faced with a scenario that Neill might possibly have gone off and become lost elsewhere. It was a possibility which, initially, could not be exclusively ruled out. They were therefore attempting to work to an impossibly poor level of information. Only later, when pieces of equipment associated with Neill were found deep in the Gully, could it be said with any certainty that they were *somewhere* down there.

The rescue attempt was not proceeding in isolation. The whole episode had caught the attention and imagination of the people of the United Kingdom and the rest of the world. Inevitably, and unfairly, questions were raised concerning this one rogue expedition among over 600 processed each year without complication. In Westminster, John Hutton, chairman of the Parliamentary Labour Party's Defence Committee, expressed his anger that soldiers' lives had been put at risk. 'When the Army is funding these exercise programmes,' he said, 'it has a responsibility to thoroughly check that they are safe.' The military defended its position, saying that adventure training exercises were 'not designed to be holidays'. A Ministry of Defence spokesman added: 'Adventure training will always have an element of risk. We do not cover our people in cotton wool.' He went on to say: 'It was a well planned and authorised expedition.' Another added: 'The best place to survive is in the jungle. There is plenty of food and water. These men have been trained to look after themselves.' Things are often not what they appear to be. Despite their combative and upbeat mood, some of the army spokesmen were privately not holding out much hope of finding the men alive. 'With every passing day and hour, the chance grows that all we will find are bodies.' This was an important factor in the rescue decision-making process. The question put quite simply was, what was an acceptable degree of risk to be set against an increasing likelihood that those being sought were dead?

So much depended upon so little information. The best source was among the five who had forced themselves out at the bottom of the Gully. 'It is not commonly realised,' said Schumacher,

> how vital Brittan's input was in rescuing the five. His eloquence and clear descriptions of what had happened were essential in the formulation of our plans. He drove himself like a human dynamo, which is remarkable when we remember the ordeal he had been through. He went about his business quietly organising. He really drove himself over that initial period when we were setting up and then, gradually, when our dependence upon him declined, when the mantle of leadership eased, then, and only then, he collapsed. We got him into hospital where he rested for two days. That man deserved a medal: there is no doubt in my mind that he saved the lives of Page and Shearer and was also instrumental in the saving of Neill's group.

(Some years previously, Brittan had been sent to his Corps' Potential Officer Cadet wing for evaluation as potential officer material. He was rejected for not displaying the requisite qualities of leadership.)

21 March saw the first improvement of the weather as the monsoon conditions abated. Group 1 was able to spend the day putting the safety ropes in position on either side of the col before returning to Panar Laban at the end of the day. This simplified the transit over this difficult ground, but perhaps more importantly, it made it safer. Simultaneously, RAF men were up in the Sikorsky helicopter reconnoitring between the 7,000 and 12,000-foot contours. The Royal Malaysian Airforce helicopter pilot, Flight Lieutenant Gabriel Joel, found the unusually fair weather conditions permitted him, his crew and the RAF observers to get a good aerial view of the Gully and the water situation. 'From the air, the water level looked manageable and we believed it would be possible to lower search and rescue workers into the area when conditions were right.' Joel's mission began at 12,000 ft, but so fickle were the weather conditions that his later attempt to go up the Gully from 2,000 ft was checked at 5,000 feet by a low cloud base.

On 22 March, both mountain rescue groups made an early start from Panar Laban in the improved weather. The pre-placing of the fixed ropes now repaid their dividend as the teams made their rapid progress, stopping off at their pre-assigned positions. Two remained at Panar Laban, four were located at the col to operate the radio link and provide support, six remained on the top abseil section for safety cover and support. This enabled the lead group of four to get down to 8,500 ft in the Gully with sufficient remaining daylight. As they penetrated deeper, it became clear that the going would continue to be difficult. There were also logistical problems. In order to climb back out after their search and maintain an acceptable safety margin, more rope was required. During this reconnaissance, a bivouac site with two empty sardine cans and a food bag bearing Neill's name were found. This was the first concrete evidence to prove that Neill and the other four were somewhere below, in the Gully. Moreover, after some ration packs found by the Malaysian search party at the bottom of the Gully were identified as having been associated with Brittan's group, it seemed reasonably certain that Neill's group had not left the Gully.

On 23 March, two members of the support team took a further 500 ft of rope down to the lead searchers. This rope enabled them to advance a further one and a half miles and another 2,200 ft down the Gully. Another bivouac site was found, and here were two more sardine cans and some rope. By now, the team was becoming over-extended over worsening terrain. Warrant Officer Haveron wrote in his report: 'The lead party reached the lowest point in the Gully which they are prepared to go to in the interest of safety at 6,300 ft.' It was here that they were confronted by a full flowing and massive 400-foot waterfall which they began to negotiate before reaching a point at which they could not proceed further forward. 'They then retreated to the support group in the dark, arriving back at 8.30pm to spend the night in a river bed bivouac site. On the 24th, all groups returned from the Gully to Panar Laban where they rested overnight.'

The RAF Mountain Rescue Team had done all that was humanly possible within their capabilities. Their penetration of the Gully from the top, together with the Malaysian search going on below, meant it was possible to predict to within one mile where Neill's group was. The trick lay in pinpointing and extracting them. Robert New had followed the details of the RAF men's progress with great interest.

'Then it suddenly occurred to me,' he said, 'that the slopes we had scrambled down in the dry weather were now raging torrents of water. Even so, I believe that they had reached to within 100–200 yards of Neill and his people.' Haveron's men's tasks did not end there, for they volunteered to provide safety support for the second phase of the British rescue operation. The requirement placed on the Ministry of Defence was for men with climbing expertise and experience of operating in a jungle environment. The group comprised 12 specialists and three potholing experts from the Army School of Adventurous Training in Ripon. Serious consideration was given to the possibility of a revised top–down approach put forward by the potholers, but the logistic tail which that plan involved and, by implication, the delay it would cause, meant that the idea was shelved. The emphasis had to be to press on, utilising the fastest possible means. Speed was of the essence.

At the base of the Gully, the Malaysian troops had been engaged in the search for a week. On Wednesday 23 March, Major General John Foley, Commander British Forces Hong Kong, arrived at the state capital. For the Malaysians in particular, his arrival coincided with a time when difficult decisions had to be made. Brigadier Hussin respected and understood the necessity of the RAF's withdrawal, but it complicated the satisfactory completion of his mission. In continuing with the search, he knew he was putting both his men's lives and his career on the line, but he recognised that the lives of the missing men were dependent on his brigade's efforts. It proved to be the most difficult decision of his life. Should he go on, or not? The Brigadier and his officers conducted regular reviews of the situation. The medical officer played a key role for, all the while, Brigadier Hussin questioned him: 'Is there a possibility of these men still being alive?' For as long as the doctor's response was not negative, there remained the stimulation to keep the searchers in place. 'Re-ration the troops for a further ten days. We will continue the search,' he ordered. Of the Britons, he said: 'We will bring them back whether they be alive, injured or dead, but we will definitely bring them out. If we had thought negatively,' he continued, 'we would have sought permission to stop the search, but we are dedicated to the saving of those people and therefore we will go on.'

For both the British and Malaysian governments the cost of the rescue operation was escalating dramatically. At the end of the affair, the Malaysian government did not pass its costs on to London for settlement. For the Malaysians, helicopter utilisation alone proved extremely costly. The Malaysians justified having helicopters on round-the-clock standby in order to take advantage of sudden breaks in the weather. The Brigadier saw in his helicopters a means of communicating with the men lost below, so that through the noise of their engines they would convey the message that people were out there trying to help, that they had not been abandoned, that their rescuers were still there. Even in the dry season, at the intermediate level, there is an almost persistent cloud formation encircling the mountain. This meant that flying outside the 6.00–8.30am bracket was almost impossible, and when conducted, highly dangerous. It also impeded any systematic grid square examination of the Gully and its surrounds. In order to take advantage of rare gaps in the clouds, helicopters and crews were kept on in Sabah and were denied permission to return to their base at Labuan. 'The Royal Malaysian Airforce,' said Brigadier Hussin, 'took the greatest risks one can think of.' That view was certainly supported by Colonel Schumacher.

He said that there was no clear perception of the lengths to which the Malaysians went to provide assistance. 'They did incredible things with their helicopters,' he said. He described having been in a helicopter heading into the Gully with 100 per cent power on:

> You had to make a run at the Gully, fly in, do your aerial survey before being blown back out of it. The downdraught pushed us out at a descent rate of 250 feet a minute. You see, the Gully is a five mile long wind tunnel. Hot air comes up from the jungle and meets the cold air rolling down the mountain at the intermediate levels.

In sport, it is often the case that the timely arrival of a substitute has an immediate impact upon the fortunes of the game. What was being played out in Low's Gully was no sport, no game, but the introduction of the relief team had a dramatic effect upon the course of the rescue. Of the five out on the mountain, Neill had weakened considerably and Chow was suffering the effects of the injury to his back, and malnutrition. Wills had been written. The other two Chinese were also malnourished and languid. The one exception, the one man with residual energy, was the formerly large man of the group, now a very much slimmed-down Major Foster.

Sporadic helicopter activity in their vicinity was observed on 21 March. From that date, Neill's group maintained a helicopter watch. They could hear helicopter activity from first light on Friday 25

March, and at 7.15am a helicopter circled above them. Frantically, Foster flashed his camera at the aircraft, convinced that the pilot had seen him but, to the dismay of all, the helicopter moved away. At mid-morning, Captain Izhar Hassan was in the air in an Alouette with three members of the relief team, in the process of reconnoitring possible insertion points. Down at Kevin's Cave, the improving weather meant that wood was dry enough to permit a fire to be lit. Coming up the valley at 6,000 ft, now temporarily clear of cloud, the pilot's and crew's attention was caught by the flash of Foster's camera. Then they saw the SOS sign, with two men lying on boulders and three others waving to attract attention. Neill, inside his sleeping bag, noted the helicopter's engine tone change. 'I was out of my sleeping bag in a jiffy – before, it would have taken longer.'

Izhar took the helicopter in close, down to 5,000 ft. It was 10.10am. 'It's them!' someone on board shouted excitedly. Someone else got out a notebook and scribbled a message. With great difficulty, Izhar held the helicopter a few feet above Neill's group while, all the time, natural forces conspired to try to tear the aircraft away. Two yellow bags were lowered by nylon cord from the helicopter to the now animated and elated men. Inside were a radio, medical supplies, and rations. What cheered Neill and Foster was the fact that they were British rations, which meant that if the UK Ministry of Defence was involved, then their families would soon be aware that they were alive and well. The note said simply: 'Hang on in there everybody.' By now low on fuel, the helicopter flew off. Those on the ground tucked into the snack food while the more substantial meal of 'boil-in-the-bag' corned beef hash and chicken casserole heated up on the stove. Meanwhile, Izhar radioed back to Headquarters with the news. Brittan, who was in the 5 Brigade Operations Room with Schumacher, was by that stage convinced that it would be a question of pulling bodies out. 'Frankly, I didn't rate their chances. I was amazed by the news, it was brilliant, and a great relief.' The news spread quickly around the world, bringing particular comfort to the families and friends of the five. Izhar returned shortly and lowered a member of the relief team who was also a paramedic.

In the meantime, the Royal Malaysian Airforce's medical rescue team, led by Major Samsuddin, was alerted and took off in Flight Lieutenant Joel's 30-seat Sikorsky Nuri helicopter. Neill and Foster insisted that in the UK this helicopter was known as a Sea King (which is manufactured by Westlands). They arrived on the scene at

10.55am. They failed to get in at the first attempt, but on the second attempt, hovering precariously between the ridges, they managed to lower two airforce medics. The downdraught from the big helicopter sent loose objects on the ground, marker panels and helmets, flying off into the air. Once the medics were on the ground, Joel took his helicopter up and out of danger, returning the remainder of the medical team to the forward landing site. Just before 3pm Joel was back, with Major Samsuddin aboard to start the process of lifting the soldiers out. The medical team on the ground had sorted the five into priorities for evacuation, the first two being Neill and Lam. Neill's protestations that, as the leader, he should go last were ignored. 'It was very precarious,' said the pilot, 'we had to hold the heli still for about 20 minutes before we could pull the duo up.' It was a long time for the pilot to concentrate, watching the action on the ground and his rotor blades whirling between the ridges of the Gully. What also caught his attention, and something he commented upon later, was that 'when we went down to 100 ft, one of the five was even taking pictures'. The helicopter crew managed to winch up Neill and then Lam on the wire-framed stretcher. According to Joel, they both managed to utter 'thank you'. 'They looked weak but generally OK.' Further attempts to lift out the others at 4pm and 5.45pm had to be abandoned due to low cloud and the onset of darkness.

Back at the Sabah Medical Centre in Kota Kinabalu, the medical staff were on standby, awaiting the arrival of Joel's helicopter. A number of the press had also foregathered and saw the big helicopter touch down. First out was Major Samsuddin to help the two out of the helicopter and onto stretchers. First Neill, then Lam, were hurried into the medical centre. Looking weak, gaunt and frail, Neill still had the spirit to give the thumbs up sign to the assembled photographers. All the time he was trapped between the two waterfalls he had been haunted by the prospect that the advance group had not survived the rain and the Gully. It was a heavy burden for any leader to bear. When the relief team medic came down and told him that they were safe and had raised the alarm, Neill said: 'It took every last scrap of my energy away.' No longer did he have five men's lives on his conscience.

At 7am the following day, Joel returned to Kevin's Cave to complete the second part of a mission he described as 'the toughest rescue mission I have ever experienced in my life.' It was a two-phase mission: the first part was to extract Foster and the two remaining

Chinese, the second to return to pick up the Malaysian and British paramedics who had stayed with the trio overnight. The only things left behind were three bergen rucksacks. Joel took the Nuri in to about 80ft above the soldiers. 'It was not easy to get close to them,' admitted Joel,

> I had wind problems, clouds blocking our view, and the Gully was very narrow . . . any slight wind change could have sent us crashing into the ridges . . . me and my crew are proud to be able to help rescue the British soldiers.

Brigadier Hussin announced that:

> The success of the operation was due to the magnificent co-operation given by all involved; the Malaysian and British armies, the Royal Malaysian Airforce and the Royal Air Force, Police Field Force, Border Scouts, Park Wardens, medical authorities, villagers and locals who helped along the way.

The fact that the rescue coincided with the peak of the period of political frigidity between the Malaysian and British governments (arising from the Pergau Dam scheme and associated claims of corruption made by a British Sunday newspaper) had absolutely no influence on events out on the ground. Both the Malaysian and British armed forces handled the task as professional people seeking to help their own kind in distress. The great strength of the soldier is that he can also be a diplomat, whereas a diplomat cannot be a soldier. Prime Minister John Major made no reference to the Pergau Dam affair when he wrote to Malaysia's Premier, Dr Mahathir, expressing his joy that the men had been found alive. He thanked Dr Mahathir for 'pulling out all stops' in a successful rescue in which the help given by the Malaysians was exemplary. In Hong Kong, Governor Chris Patten was particularly pleased with the news of the rescue, issuing a statement congratulating all who had been involved in 'what has been an extraordinarily difficult rescue operation.'

Neill scanned the press cuttings brought to him by Schumacher, who warned him of the acute media interest that had been stimulated by his ordeal. Neill's position, and his future, must have been uppermost in his mind. What Brittan had said at his press interview twelve days after emerging from the jungle but prior to Neill and his group being found, had not therefore been of great help to Neill. But what had Brittan said that was untrue? He said that the expedition had been plagued by mishap from the start; he expressed his pride in defeating the Gully, but admitted that there had been differences in levels of fitness within the group. Where he might have veered away from the whole truth it was entirely to Neill's benefit. He said he believed the team had embarked upon the expedition properly prepared and equipped. He said the kit was so heavy that to carry radio equipment would have been difficult, and it would have been uncertain whether they would have been able to contact anyone. It was on the basis of this press briefing that Foster insisted that selling his account to the media would help to put his side of the story.

What is of interest in Neill's and Foster's book is the way in which genuine questions regarding the team's preparedness are mentioned almost incidentally and then explained away in an unconvincing manner. We have spoken about radios. There is then the question of directional beacons, about which Neill apparently told the Board he had no idea as to their availability. Foster introduces the topic in the book. He tells how a specialist told him that search and rescue beacons which transmit by satellite are accurate to only three kilometres. The expert was also alleged to have told him that when not working to satellites, beacons only work to line of sight and would therefore have limited utility in the Gully.

The SARBE (Search and Rescue Beacon) is a single channel UHF radio which transmits on the distress frequency. It is line of sight and includes a ground to air radio facility. A search and rescue aircraft flying up and down the valley would be able to take a fix on the SARBE transmission and, by repeating the operation once or twice, would achieve a convergence of bearings indicating where the party was. The signal penetrates foliage and could have been used inside the Gully. However, this system does not work to satellites.

What Foster's expert seems to have been discussing, or was said to have been discussing, sounds like the Global Positioning System or GPS. What is needed here is three satellites within the party's usual horizon – something which is not thought to have been possible in the Gully.

With the right equipment, Neill's group could have determined their position almost to within a foot but, in order to communicate that information to rescuers, they would have needed a second piece of equipment – namely a radio. The homework had not been done thoroughly before or after the expedition.

Schumacher said that one of his abiding memories was that of an emaciated Foster, by the door of the helicopter, filming the world's press as the helicopter came in. The wonder was that the battery was still functioning, but then Foster had only been able to use two of the films he had brought on the expedition. 'I never gave up,' Foster told the waiting pressmen. 'I am looking forward to seeing my family back home – I am a bit more hungry than I normally am.' None of them had been long on the ground before bids began to arrive from the media vying with one another for exclusive rights to the soldiers' stories. Thus far, the lid had been kept on the details of the expedition, except for the very general conference at which Brittan, chaperoned by Public Relations people, was able to give a bare outline. Public Relations encouraged the soldiers to speak with one voice, for already the press had formed a number of newsworthy notions. Among these was the suggestion of a delay in starting the rescue operation, and Neill's leadership qualities were also a matter of intense speculation. The attempt to ensure that the men acted together failed. Robert New recalled visiting the five in hospital. 'The notes were already coming in', he said. Schumacher commented upon the avalanche of press offers. It was something he could not and did not wish to handle. Believing it best for Foster to appoint his own solicitor, Schumacher gave him the name of a person in the London firm of Swepstone Walsh. Accordingly, Foster put the call through to wake Patrick Stewart his solicitor in the middle of the night.

New recalled that:

> Ron Foster was particularly keen to have his video batteries recharged in order to show his videos. I remember the BBC man seeing them and saying, 'The film you've got here is dynamite. You must realise that there's a lot of political sensitivity here.' I've no doubt what he meant was that the rescue had cost the Malaysian government a considerable amount of money. If they (the five) made money out of the rescue, how would the Malaysian authorities feel about it?

Brittan remembered meeting Foster in hospital on the day of his rescue. Referring to his videos, Brittan recalled him saying: 'This is dynamite, we've got to talk'. His attitude appeared to shock Neill who, Brittan said, distanced himself from Foster's intentions. 'OK Ron – another time.' Any feeling Brittan had had for Foster from that point on turned to instant dislike. When, during the course of his interview for this book, Neill was asked to verify that this event had indeed taken place, Neill replied: 'You will have to talk to Ron about that, you see he and I became very close when we were stuck together in the Gully'. When Foster was approached for his series of interviews, he said 'I have heard of you' and declined to be interviewed, saying that he would not do so until after his book had been published. After the publication of *SOS*, when contacted again, he said he would 'have to think about it', but promised he would contact the author within seven days with his decision. He did not.

6
Reflections

When Mann and Mayfield heard the excellent news of the rescue of Neill's group, they were in different hospitals in Plymouth. Both had had an eventful return home. They were met off the aircraft at Hong Kong's Kai Tak airport by an ambulance and some minders and taken to the officers' mess at the Composite Ordnance Depot. There to meet them was Lieutenant Colonel D J Kerr, commanding officer of Cheung, Chow and Lam. Before their debriefing began they were asked whether they would like anything to eat. Mann ordered steak, egg and chips. It was not long before he was taken very, very ill. After recounting what had happened in Sabah, both men were removed to the British Military Hospital in Kowloon where their injuries and sickness were treated according to priority. It was on Day 3 that the interest in the story of Mann's hand developed until it burst out into the international press. There was by now sustained press interest in the pair, so much so that women of the press, bearing flowers and fruit and pretending to be wives, sisters or girlfriends, presented themselves at the Reception Desk downstairs. As soon as they were fit enough to be moved, Hong Kong's military thankfully put them on an aircraft for London.

Plain clothes policemen met them at Heathrow, guiding them through a labyrinth of tunnels to a room where they were received by Colonel O T Hall, Neill's superior officer, and Major Tom Parker, Commandant of the Army Adventure Training School at Ripon. Their wives waited in an adjoining room. After a further debriefing, both were allowed to head homeward to Plymouth accompanied by their respective families. Their wives had been forewarned that both men had lost a great deal of weight. Of the two, Mann was in the worst state; his wife cried that night. Already the malaria was working within the soldiers' bodies and they became weaker and weaker, losing their appetites and suffering intermittent shivering accompanied by heavy bouts of perspiration. The first doctor called to see Mann did not recognise the symptoms, but Mann knew he had contracted malaria. Following a tumble downstairs, he told his wife to ring the Territorial Army Centre. As a result of that call, his own doctor hurried round and, on seeing him, called an ambulance.

In the Sabah Medical Centre the exhausted Neill and Lam had recovered well after a good night's rest. After the other three had been brought in, their doctor described their condition as 'good though weak'. He found them to be free of disease, although he reserved his position vis-à-vis malaria as its symptoms only appear later. They were able to walk about in the Centre, sustained by a liquid diet, porridge and ice cream. 'If they eat heavy meals now,' explained their consultant surgeon, 'they will suffer vomiting and other symptoms as their stomachs over the last few weeks have shrunk.'

On 27 March, Neill, Foster, Cheung, Chow and Lam, fit enough to travel, were joined by Brittan to fly to Hong Kong and London respectively. On the same flight were members of the relief team. At Kota Kinabalu airport, Neill told the press that Kinabalu still remained a challenge for him. 'I would still like to come back another day to conquer it.' Then he said, which will be a relief to some: 'I will personally not do it the same way we did.' After thanking those responsible for their rescue, he also thanked the five who had preceded him for raising the alarm. He said he felt that the expedition had been a justifiable challenge, meeting all the criteria of army adventure training, and that his team's experience could usefully provide others who would follow with the information which would enable them to accomplish what his team had failed to achieve.

The previous day, in Hong Kong, Major General John Foley addressed the subject of adventurous training, defending this type of exercise as being essential in building character in fighting men. 'Our soldiers' performance in the Gulf or the Falklands would, I would suggest, have been much less good if we'd actually given up doing these sorts of exercises.' Adventure training, he said, 'develops people's initiatives. It hardens them and makes them able to react to adverse conditions. I would wish that they continue.' The General spoke of an Inquiry. He confirmed that an Inquiry would be held in the United Kingdom to investigate why the soldiers had gone missing, but he advised that the results might never be made public. Ultimately, only the Board's outline findings were released.

On their arrival in Hong Kong, Neill and Foster were told that whilst in Hong Kong they were not to talk to the press without military Public Relations agreement. The survivors were admitted to the BMH (British Military Hospital) for physical check-ups and mental monitoring. A high profile press conference took place. In the meantime, the army flew Mrs Neill and Mrs Foster to Hong Kong to be reunited with their husbands. Some press people made a point of finding out which plane the wives were travelling on and went to Hong Kong on the same flight. The contacts which various British national media representatives established with Mrs Neill and Mrs Foster on the Hong Kong-bound flight were the catalyst for the subsequent agreements made between the parties. Of the press conference, one observer said that 'the Hong Kong media in full cry, in particular the photographers, make Britain's Royal Rat Pack seem like a group of choirboys on a Sunday School outing by comparison'. The whole thrust of the Hong Kong Headquarters staff was to provide all possible assistance to two fellow officers and three locally-enlisted soldiers who, less than 48 hours previously, had been close to death, and, as importantly, to their families who were also being harassed by the media.

It is apparent that some additional liaison with the press did take place in the BMH but there were no Public Relations people present. Neill presented highlights from Foster's video in such a manner as to suggest he was auctioning it. The BBC's man present cautioned Neill that the video was perishable, the more it was run through a video, so its broadcast quality would be marred. He recommended that the video should be sent to London as soon as possible, even though the auction had not been concluded. Neill, his hand clutching a cellular telephone, accepted the advice and the Betamax cassettes, accompanied by a third party as 'minder', set off for the BBC's bureau in Hong Kong. There they were copied to U-Matic to be couriered to London to await collection by the winner of the auction. The BBC's offer of £25,000 for exclusive world rights was to be overtaken by the bid of a private company.

Major and Mrs Foster flew home from Hong Kong on 30 March, the same day that Cheung and Lam were released from hospital. Lieutenant Colonel and Mrs Neill flew home the next day, 1 April 1994. The authorities may have been congratulating themselves on having conducted a smooth, uncomplicated operation, yet there were three separate eruptions waiting in the wings. The consequences of eruptions such as those about to make their mark are that they so trouble Chiefs of the General Staff as to cause them to reach for their telephones to trouble their immediate subordinates, who in turn perpetuate the expressions of displeasure down the chain of command. Prevention is preferable to the cure.

Many members of Hong Kong's public, as well as the media, found it difficult to comprehend why three local soldiers, employed to all intents and purposes for administrative and supporting duties exclusively in Hong Kong, should be 'on duty' on a mountain in Borneo. That was as much due to the endemic lack of understanding of how the military operates as anything else. The Hong Kong media's championing of the cause of local soldiers was due to the simple natural instinct to support the home team as well as to keep what had been one of the biggest stories for many months going. The participation of Hong Kong Chinese soldiers on adventure training expeditions such as that held in Sabah attracted the attention of professional critics and gave it a political profile it did not deserve.

On 4 and 5 April 1994, the London *Daily Mail* identified itself as the winner of the 'auction' for Foster's otherwise unavoidably mundane diary. The record was published in two parts. It did not take long for Foster's criticism (see page 96) of the three Chinese team members to hit the Hong Kong press. There was understandable dismay and even outrage within the Territory; a situation reflected in the editorial of the *Eastern Express,* headed 'Conduct Definitely Unbecoming'. The newspaper suggested that the 'derision and the criticism' must have struck a hard blow to the three soldiers who had barely escaped with their lives. 'Neill, it must be stressed,' ran the editorial,

> was the man obsessed with the idea of a descent into the most dangerous route of Mount Kinabalu ... first impressions suggest the whole expedition was misconceived and should never have been sanctioned.

The newspaper then observed that only one side of the story had been released:

> Apart from Foster's account, we have no means of knowing how the Hong Kong soldiers behaved ... however, we have some idea about basic human decency. Such a concept does not include bad-mouthing colleagues in the most public way after they have narrowly escaped

> death. The word honour used to have some meaning among the British officer class.

Major General John Foley quickly interceded by taking the highly unusual step of issuing a public statement to pay tribute to Cheung's, Chow's and Lam's 'dignity, restraint and fortitude'. Implicit in what was a genuine expression of praise, confidence and admiration, was an official contradiction of what Foster had said. The local media were clearly watching to see whether the 'top brass' would support the three local men or the two UK-based officers who they suspected as being blameworthy. The General's quick and reasoned response defused what could well have become an ugly situation. Hong Kong's military were incensed at what Foster, an outsider, had done and were determined that the Chinese soldiers should not be used as undeserved scapegoats. Lance Corporal (now Mr) Cheung was particularly distressed by the incorrect and misleading comments and threatened to sue:

> We didn't give any problems. I don't understand why he made these remarks. They found us fit and selected us to take part in the exercise. But now he says we were a liability to them. I was the first to abseil from Lone Tree into the jungle. Is that the action of a child? Yes, there were times when one or another felt weak, but that was also true of Neill and Foster. We were not experienced enough to abseil on our own. However, we never required the equipment to be checked except for the first abseil. There were occasions when Neill did not trust the belays left by Mayfield and he would move them. That worried us because Mayfield was the expert.

Cheung's point was well made. Neill had established the loose criteria for their selection and when, with good reason, the Chinese soldiers questioned the wisdom of that selection, their observations were set aside. Foster also accused the Chinese of having dumped rations. The reasonable counter which Cheung put before the subsequent Inquiry was that if they had dumped rations, why were they not found? The Board found to its satisfaction that the Chinese had not dumped rations. All in all, the Foster diaries, in which he expressed a personal not a factual view of his Chinese subordinates, had been a pretty sordid episode. It wasn't so much the unwarranted attack on individuals but that the diary containing the attacks attracted a financial reward.

Cheung considered suing Foster for what he had written. He was deeply embarrassed, hurt and angry about what his superior had blurted out to the press. 'I was going to take him to court, but the Army Legal Officer said it was a personal thing and I would have difficulties if I tried.' The Army Legal Officer in Hong Kong was ex-Sandhurst, ex-Brigade of Guards, Lieutenant Colonel Richard Spencer, an English solicitor. His client was Major General Foley but he also gave legal counselling to Cheung and Foster – that is, legal comment to listen to, to consider, but not rely upon. The army lawyer said without reserve that there is always a problem with advising all the sides of a polygon. He told Cheung not to expect legal aid for defamation suits which are expensive. He also told the other ranks that if any of them had any complaint about the preparation or conduct of the expedition, then they would be wise to save their stories for the Board of Inquiry (which he was sure would come) rather than give them to the press there and then, which would provide a good opportunity for the lawyer of the criticised party to prepare his questions.

There seems little doubt that had the Commander British Forces been able to order Foster not to sell his videos he would have done so. Richard Spencer recollected how the videos had been the major media interest. 'The videos' value was ebbing; the diary was valueless without the videos, but I confess that my recollection is that I was unaware of the diary.' It appears that at the time, the Joint Services Public Relations team was also unaware of the existence of Foster's diary. Spencer remarked how the account that he had briefed General Foley prior to Neill's and Foster's arrival in the Territory was incorrect:

> I was on local leave at the time and met the two officers at the British Military Hospital after their arrival there. It was after that meeting that I advised General Foley. I did say that I thought it would not be a lawful command to order Foster not to sell his videos. I said further that I thought the applicability of Crown Copyright could be argued either way. But I questioned why we should wish to claim Crown Copyright. There being no obvious answer, I recommended that Ron should be allowed to keep it.

The diary was infinitely more controversial than the videos. It was not that the contents of the diary had been seen, but rather it reflected an attitude that in view of what had gone before, profiteering would be inappropriate. However, although Foster was subject to military law, he was nevertheless a civilian soldier whose profession was as a financial adviser. Within the regular officer corps it has long been the custom and practice not to deal directly with the press without clearance. In fact Queen's Regulations as expanded in Defence Council Instructions establishes the procedure to be followed. But then, Foster's diary was his own and he used the camera given to him by his wife and his own video. As mentioned, there was no certainty that Crown Copyright could be imposed. Moreover, it has to be remembered that the offers put to Foster for his video were of a perishable nature – £40,000–£50,000 on Friday 25 March had shrunk to £20,000–£30,000 on Monday 28 March 1994. Any imposed delay might have resulted in someone of that mind suing for loss of earnings. Although Neill's name was associated with Foster's, the totality of his involvement in these deals is unclear. The evidence is that he was actively involved in attempting to accrue his share. Richard Spencer recalled how, shortly after Neill and Foster reached the BMH:

> I returned to my office to be asked to ring Neill at the BMH. I did so and he asked me to find him in Hong Kong a media lawyer who could draft a partnership agreement to tie Foster and his video in with Neill's story so that Foster couldn't sell his video to the eclipse of Neill's bit. I spoke with the Attorney General's department and was given the name of two solicitors which I passed to Neill. What he did I don't know. I doubt much, if anything.

The draft Agreement between the *Daily Mail* and Major and Mrs Foster does reveal, however, that the Fosters were being asked to accept that Neill should exclusively assist the *Daily Mail* in connection with the publication of Foster's story.

This delicate matter was given a light gloss in the officers' book. Neill admits that he, as a Regular officer, should not exploit his predicament, but they convinced themselves that Foster could exploit his predicament by taking money from the press. They recount how Foster had heard 'officially' that, if he were to sell his story, it would be a good idea to donate a substantial amount of the tens of thousands of pounds he would make to the Malaysian rescue effort. As a beneficiary of his largesse, the name of the Malaysian Red Crescent was regularly repeated. Apparently he thought this a good idea. In due course he was given 'every encouragement and assistance' by 'various officials' to sell the controversial diary to the *Daily*

Mail. Efforts were made to identify these helpful 'officials', but to no avail. 'It certainly was not me,' said Schumacher, 'I had no such authority and besides, I did not go on to Hong Kong with them.' The details of Foster's terrible accusation were not repeated in the book. This might seem defensible, but the failure to take the opportunity to apologise for the acute loss of face suffered by the three young Chinese is inexcusable. 'Now', said Cheung,

> we have to contend with the book which I feel blames the three of us. But there is nothing we can do. Some of our friends have made comments doubting our abilities. This really does not make us look good in the eyes of our families and friends.

One outstanding question is if, as Foster said, the Ministry of Defence was 'quite happy' with the book, why did it cause offence to the other members of the expedition? 'Happiness' is a difficult condition to contemplate in the context of the Ministry of Defence, but a Department of State will examine a book such as Neill's and Foster's against different criteria from those of the participants or average reader. When such a book has passed through the normal clearance system in the Ministry of Defence, the expression 'happy' means that there are no security breaches in the book and that there is nothing which will cause Foreign Policy difficulties for the Government. There is again the point that all Expedition members gave evidence on oath before the Board of Inquiry. The text clearance would also have to ensure that there were no contradictions between what was said to the Board and what appeared in the book. Essentially it is a review to ensure that perjury has not been committed. Otherwise, all the facts, opinions and interpretations in the book are entirely those of the authors and not a proper area for the Ministry of Defence to comment upon.

The moral and ethical objections to what Foster had done in capitalising on his rescue were deep-seated. A consensus view was that the saving of his life had been as big as rewards come. To derive financial advantage when the state of Malaysia, a developing country, had spared no expense to rescue him and his colleagues, was seen as an affront to the British military ethos. After all, ethics and the maintenance of those ethics are a *sine qua non* of leadership. On 6 April 1994, Foster was at Headquarters Eastern District, York in connection with the press conference to be held there the next day. There he was interviewed by a senior officer in a meeting which lasted for some hours and concluded with an agreement by Foster to distribute part of the proceeds from his various deals to the Malaysian rescue services. It will be recalled that when rescued he thought this to have been a 'good idea'. As a temporary expedient, the undisclosed sum of money is believed to have been put into a separate account with a view to Major and Mrs Foster disbursing the said amount in Malaysia at a later date. The details of that agreement in principle were announced in public.

The Army held its first UK post-rescue press conference at York on Wednesday 6 April 1994. In view of the publication of Foster's diary, it was an important event to demonstrate to the domestic and international press that the expedition was conducted both well and harmoniously. Neill and Brittan had been practised the day before on answers to the anticipated, predictable questions. Both the officer and the non-commissioned officer gave their own uncontroversial accounts of what had happened. At question time, Neill was bombarded with questions: Did he lose control? Had there been friction between the two groups? Rather than tell the press they would have to wait until the Board of Inquiry's findings were promulgated, Neill had a momentary lapse of concentration: 'Personally, I am extremely angry that half of my expedition proceeded on down Low's Gully without my authorisation.' Brittan, sitting nearby, looked visibly stunned. In their book there is an interesting line: 'When reporters heard this, they assumed that he was attacking Brittan, who was sitting next to him'.

As the *Sunday Times* reported:

> It was meant to be a celebration of heroism, a chance for the men who tackled Low's Gully and survived a month in one of the most inhospitable places on earth to retell a story worthy of Rider Haggard.

Instead, therefore, of emphasising:

> the bravery and clearheadedness of the typical British officer in a difficult and dangerous situation ... the ill-fated trip through the Malaysian jungles and mountains turned into a public relations disaster.

However Brittan stayed calm and close to the script. 'Until all the information is in, we should not go shooting anyone,' he said.

After the press had dispersed, the Headquarters' shell-shocked staff confronted Neill to account for his action. He told them that he did not want to say anything that he had not said to BBC TV. Being unaware he had said anything to BBC TV, they sought urgent clarification of what he meant. Apparently, when he arrived back in Yorkshire he had been offered two rooms in the officers' mess for himself and his family, to afford him breathing space from the predictable press attention. Understandably he wanted to go home, to be with his family, but this did expose him to constant, wearing press harassment. One reporter from BBC TV, an apparently benign, grandfatherly figure with grey hair, was among those to ask for an interview, to which Neill acceded. 'That was an error of judgement,' admitted Neill. 'I was promised and agreed to an interview on survival. I did it off my back. I was set up.' This interview is not mentioned in the book.

The interview was broadcast on the evening of the press conference. It was an interview for which he was manifestly neither ready nor prepared. It was too soon after his ordeal, a confusion of faith and reality, seemingly as a Christian hoping the lions would be kindred spirits. The interviewer put to him a wide range of questions. One question revealed where the programme fitted into the pecking order of objective journalism. Had there been discussion of cannibalism and what had been the Colonel's position on the subject? Neill was on record as having talked of such things with the Chinese soldiers at Kevin's Cave, 'to jolt them along'. He had said they would die when he told them to die and once they were dead they would not be worth eating. On a higher plane, the BBC had enlisted the distinguished conqueror of Everest, Lord Hunt, to comment separately upon the expedition. You 'have to look at leadership at the centre of the problem', said Lord Hunt. It was 'an object lesson on how not to conduct such an expedition . . . way outside the bounds of safety'. As to the absence of radios and flares, that was 'sheer criminal negligence'. The negative impact of the programme was evident after it had been put together and broadcast. It was not the stuff to impress the army's hierarchy.

The Board of Inquiry, comprising four officers, duly assembled at York on 25 April 1994. It was to investigate the planning, preparation and conduct of the exercise. By implication, 'conduct' also means misconduct, and it was therefore a function of the Board to determine whether charges should be laid against any of the individuals concerned. With the exception of Chow who was in hospital, the nine assembled at York for the gathering of the necessary evidence on oath. This Board of Inquiry was not like a civil court where the witnesses give their evidence separately. In York, the nine heard all the evidence and had the opportunity to question members of their own team and others called to give evidence. Thus, although the detailed findings were not published, it was possible, through the process of targeted interviewing, to put the pieces of the jigsaw together. The Board sat until 24 May and included visits to Sabah and Hong Kong where it concluded its business.

There is a dichotomy here. That is, between the function of a Board whose primary aim is to gather the facts of a complex event diligently yet with due expedition, and yet also to exercise vigilance in identifying misconduct. If, for example, the President and members of the Board took the view that any of the soldiers' conduct had been to the prejudice of good order and military discipline by virtue of disloyalty or, worse, disobedience, or that the officers had been negligent in their duties, then the Board would have had to be halted in each case to allow for an investigation by the Special Investigation Branch of the Royal Military Police. The evidence of a Board of Inquiry cannot be used to support charges made against an individual. The reality, therefore, was that if a long-drawn-out Inquiry was to be avoided (there was concern that there might be a 'hole' in adventure training procedures), then no severe punishments would arise as a result of the Board's findings.

For the first time ever some of the details, as opposed to the formal findings, of an internal Board of Inquiry were made public. This was a break with precedent. However, with the officers having blamed the non-commissioned officers and the Chinese soldiers for aspects of the exercise's failure, the army felt it appropriate to identify some aspects of the officers' conduct to be found wanting. The Board considered that Neill's judgement and leadership during parts of the expedition were flawed and that the decision to take the less experienced members into Low's Gully was over ambitious. The Board also formed the opinion that during the period of Neill's illness, some of the decisions taken by Foster subsequently contributed to the situation of jeopardy which developed. Neill and Foster were both subsequently interviewed by the Board's convening officer, Major General Patrick Cordingley, General Officer Commanding Eastern District. Later, Neill alone was interviewed by the Deputy Commander United Kingdom Land Forces.

The good which does emerge from such negative situations is the sensible application of lessons learned. This applies to both the specific and the general. Sabah's Tourism and Environmental Development Minister very quickly said that the Gully would not be placed off limits to adventure tourism. 'The more dangerous it is,' he said, 'the more it attracts tourists. But we have to look at things positively. Instead of stopping people challenging the Gully, it would be more appropriate to identify the danger points so that climbers who intend to explore the area are properly prepared.'

The Board did look at and recommend an upgrading of qualifications for those conducting abseiling. It did not appear to address the problem of individuals who, once qualified, remain qualified for life. The application procedure was finessed so that expeditions are now graded according to the degree of difficulty and accessibility, taking due account of British representation out on the ground. Once an application has received the commanding officer's endorsement, it is then analysed in depth by adventure training experts, with regard to difficulty, level of training, and to identify exactly what the team leader hopes to achieve. No longer are qualifications the sole enabling criteria. Also reviewed are training programmes and equipment checks.

Brigadier General Hussin was asked, in view of his recent experiences but not necessarily with Neill's expedition in mind, how should adventure training exercises be conceived and executed. The key criteria, he said, are command, control, communications and information:

> If those four are not right, there is even greater potential for difficulty. You must have contingency plans when you tackle such places as Mount Kinabalu. If you don't, you risk being caught with your pants down. In these circumstances, there are so many unknown factors. You have to respect the ground, know all about it but specifically, heed the experience and advice of experts. Respect their advice. This invariably involves timely consultation. There will be risks, but unnecessary risks can be avoided by drawing up calculated contingency plans. The command structure must be clearly laid out. The reporting procedure has to be defined and the necessary planning and preparation made, including group training. Communications are vital, as are medical and survival kits.

The Brigadier said that in his view, exercise planners have to think through the possibility of others being drawn into their exercise and involve them in contingency plans. He observed how the size of groups participating in adventurous training had become an emerging topic for debate. He believed that if all members were of similar fitness and ability then large groups should be OK, but he was inclined to prefer smaller groups in conditions such as those found in Low's Gully.

The Board of Inquiry revealed that in the Board's opinion, the planning for the expedition was conducted thoroughly and professionally. But was it? Having decided to go in heavy, would it not have been wise to ensure that the normally willowy Cantonese nominated for this exercise had the strength and stamina to carry the heavy packs? It was because they did not that Neill was obliged to institute a half load shuttle which effectively ended any prospect of all ten succeeding in getting through Low's Gully. Once on top of the mountain, it was too late to learn of shortcomings in this area. There was then the statement that 'radios do not work in Low's Gully'. None of the ten had really been in Low's Gully proper before, and yet the RAF found hand-held radios did work along the north–south aligned Gully. What then of thinking through to final conclusions? 'Flares are hazardous air cargo, therefore we cannot have flares on the exercise.' They could have been procured in Brunei or Sabah. Then, the assertion that they would not have worked in the Gully. If the flash unit on a camera operated five feet from the ground could be seen, how much more effective a flare would have been.

More than once there is evidence of the lack of a failsafe system, the working out of what to do if something went wrong, of asking 'so what?' as often as it takes to run out of answers. A large, ten-man team has to be close, it has to be bonded. Yet here at Kinabalu there were three factions: officers, non-commissioned officers, and the Chinese. Moreover, there was the coincidence of rank/types with functions, be that oldies, whippets or novices. The rank of the officers had some bearing on the complications which arose. Lieutenant Colonel and Major are really ranks too far removed from the common denominator among the men, mostly lance corporals. The application of leadership comes in many forms but, put simply, it can be exercised directly or through intermediaries. Even the most junior subaltern does not always exercise direct leadership because he has a sergeant and corporals in his platoon through whom he commands. The problem for senior officers on either side of their fiftieth birthday is the real prospect of having got out of the habit of leading directly. From the evidence available, Neill's distinct form of leadership was not suitable for adaptation into first line, direct leadership. He is a practised leader but not an outgoing extrovert who fires people up, so in this case there could be a conclusion that the leadership he provided was not of the type required. Moreover, they sought to impose a hierarchical structure when it was not needed.

A further point to ponder is that of multi-cultural working, a relatively new but increasingly important aspect of general leadership. Few of the team went out of their way to learn about the Chinese and their ways, and there was among the British soldiers an assumption that the Chinese were the same as them. This was a serious breakdown in communication for which the officers must bear some of the blame, for otherwise the rations fiasco would not have occurred. It is impossible to lead groups of mixed nationalities if the cultures involved are not understood. What this does is to confirm the absence of compatibility within the group.

Teams have to be chosen for compatibility and it is exactly that: it is choosing a team, not choosing stars. This exercise left itself with no opportunity to determine compatibility, to establish compatibility criteria, or to set standards. That there are mountain training establishments which run courses to test a team and its reserves' compatibility is not without relevance. Perhaps the overall lack of direction can be attributed to there being different agendas within the group. Understandably the officers will proclaim their commitment to adventure training but, whereas that is true of the others, was it not their personal ambition which was the core reason for this exercise, and the other eight participants merely the cladding to make it possible?

The prerequisite for success in this environment is stamina – something that is built up over a period of time, and yet there was no schedule or programme or testing of individuals. Nor was there an understanding of the relationship between success and age. What comes with age is hesitation, reflected in an inability to commit onself quite so readily. The result is the loss of the zip edge and the reason why the team broke down into two speed components, the slow group also being influenced by the presence of novices and the need to employ additional safety measures. When he returned home, Foster told his local newspaper how he had had to keep his heartbeat down and breathe regularly:

> I was not going to take any unnecessary risks, and if I did that I knew I would be OK even if it did mean it took all day to climb a mountain . . . it can take all day to go a couple of hundred yards.

It is true that the team suffered the misfortune of the heavy rains beginning on the afternoon on 1 March. But it was an eventuality about which they had been warned by New and, if they had kept to their own schedule, they would have been towards the end of the Gully before the rain fell. They were already seriously behind schedule when the rains came.

By the time officers have reached the hallowed ranks of Lieutenant Colonel and Major, towards the twilight of their careers, they are so often imbued with such a high degree of confidence as to be dismissive of the advice of others. Ambition or indeed obsession cloud both judgement and the decision-making processes. When one or more people want to do something so very badly, they can become so intensely focused upon it that advice which in any way contradicts or questions what they have made up their minds to do is set aside. There is also the tendency to obscure an individual's own self-knowledge and this can be a very serious defect because self-knowledge is at the very heart of leadership. Both Neill and Foster were twelve years older than when they had been on their last joint exercise near Low's Gully, and those 12 years make a big difference. It has been speculated that Neill was suffering from fatigue before the exercise began, leading to the conclusion: 'One feels that a non-playing administrative element, both in the mounting stage and on the ground in-theatre, would have been invaluable.'

We have to remind ourselves once again that the Low's Gully adventure was a rogue event and should not be used as an example to make hasty judgements as to the value and efficacy of adventurous training. That much was emphasised by General Cordingley at his press conference:

> Hence the importance which the army attaches to adventurous training activities, which over the past two years have involved sixty thousand soldiers on two thousand expeditions of which some one thousand two hundred have been undertaken overseas. Nothing which has come out during this Board of Inquiry has cast any doubt on the continuing value of adventurous training as a method of development for soldiers in the army and therefore our commitment to it remains as strong as ever.

Whatever action the military took to bring this chapter to an end, it always had one objective in mind – to calm things down. Once that had been done, rather like the full stops at the end of sentences, denoting the end of the matter, the General Officer Commanding Eastern District awarded Corporal Brittan, Lance Corporal Mayfield and Lance Corporal Cheung commendations for their actions during the expedition. Due recognition and praise were also given by General Cordingley to the involvement of the Armed Forces of Malaysia:

> I would like to take this opportunity to pay tribute to the magnificent efforts of the Malaysian armed forces and the assistance from the government of Malaysia which brought this rescue operation to a satisfactory conclusion.

Moreover, on 29 November 1994, at the annual banquet of the Guild of Air Pilots and Air Navigators in London, the Grand Master's commendation was presented by HRH King Hussein of Jordan to Lieutenant Gabriel Joel and three of his RMAF crew members for the rescue from Low's Gully of Lieutenant Colonel Neill, Major Foster, Lance Corporal Cheung, Private Lam and Private Chow. The flying skills and vital contribution made by the army pilot, Captain Izhar Hassan, did not receive recognition by the Guild.

Neill and Foster concluded that no member of the expedition appeared to have suffered any lasting harm, physical or mental. Mann was away from work for a year and suffers recurrent malaria. Mayfield's experience left him severely unsettled and with no confidence in the officer corps. He left the army. Of the three Chinese, only Lam remains in the army. The other two have been discharged as part of the rundown process towards 1997. Neill was to complain afterwards of Cheung's and Chow's selection for the expedition because, since they were due to leave the army, they would derive no benefit from the expedition. All three of the Chinese were promised copies of Foster's video. 'Instead,' said Cheung, 'he sold his video and diary and we got nothing'. When the BBC made their programme for the 999 Emergency series based on the Kevin's Cave party's exploits, Cheung and Chow were promised £50 each for helping with the interview. Again, they received nothing. Cheung is unemployed and Chow is on a twenty per cent disability pension which brings him HK$500 a month – less than £50. The big money went not to those who succeeded, but to one who failed and, moreover, who provided a highly selective and over-embellished account of his part in what, in fact, was an ill-conceived and, at the end, sordid venture. It seems that financially successful books are often associated with failure. *Tornado Down* and *Bravo Two Zero* come to mind. Perhaps, in the future, we shall see groups or individuals undertaking something extreme with failure as their only motive.

How, therefore, do we assess Neill and Foster? Should, or could Neill, the senior of the two and the leader, have had a restraining influence on the Major? Did he wish to? To come back to the question set at the beginning, was Foster a hero? Their book infers that to be the case. The Board of Inquiry, having heard the available evidence for a month, would have been in the best position to answer our question. 'The Board concluded,' said an official who had seen the proceedings, that:

> Foster's background was unsuitable to allow him to participate in the leadership of such an exercise. Throughout the course of the expedition, these shortcomings manifested themselves. It was very evident during the taking of evidence that the soldiers had little respect for him. They were shocked by the speed with which he sought to derive commercial advantage from their collective misfortune. I seem to remember the Board concluding that he was out of his depth handling soldiers.

Index